HOW TO RETIRE BY 40

The Complete Guide to Building $2 Million in 18 Years

How to Retire by 40: The Complete Guide to Building $2 Million in 18 Years

Copyright © 2025 by Sean Taylor

All rights reserved. No part of this publication may be reproduced, distributed, or transmitted in any form or by any means, including photocopying, recording, or other electronic or mechanical methods, without the prior written permission of the publisher, except in the case of brief quotations embodied in critical reviews and certain other noncommercial uses permitted by copyright law.

ISBN: 979-8-9930145-1-7

Print Edition: August 2025

Publisher: Sean Taylor

Printed in the United States of America

Disclaimer: The information in this book is for educational purposes only and should not be considered as financial advice. Past performance does not guarantee future results. Please consult with a qualified financial advisor before making investment decisions.

DEDICATION

To every young professional who refuses to accept that working until 65 is the only option.

Your financial freedom journey starts now.

PROLOGUE

THE CHOICE THAT CHANGES EVERYTHING

THE QUESTION THAT STARTED IT ALL

What if I told you that the biggest financial decision of your life isn't what house to buy, what car to drive, or even what career to pursue?

What if I told you that the single choice that will determine whether you work until you're 65 or retire at 40 is much simpler — and much harder — than you think?

That choice is this: **Are you willing to live like no one else today so you can live like no one else tomorrow?**

THE TALE OF TWO GRADUATES

Meet Sarah and Elliot. Both graduated from the same university in the same year with business degrees and similar student loan debt. Both landed entry-level jobs earning around $35,000. Both were 22 years old with their entire financial futures ahead of them.

Sarah's Path: The "Normal" Route

Sarah did what most college graduates do. She got a nice apartment, bought a reliable car with monthly payments, and slowly increased her lifestyle as her income grew. She saved when she could, invested in her 401(k) when her employer matched, and lived comfortably within her means.

At 40, Sarah earned $75,000 annually, had about $180,000 saved for retirement, owned a home with a mortgage, and faced another 25 years of work before she could afford to retire.

Sarah followed conventional financial wisdom—and got conventional results.

Elliot's Path: The Road Less Traveled

Elliot made a different choice. Despite earning the same starting salary as Sarah, he decided to live like a broke college student while investing like a millionaire. He kept his expenses minimal, maximized his savings rate, and aggressively built multiple income streams through real estate, business ownership, and strategic investments.

At 40, Elliot had a net worth of $2.2 million, generated $337,000 annually in passive income, and had complete control over how he spent his time.

Elliot chose the unconventional path—and got unconventional results.

THE MATH THAT MOST PEOPLE IGNORE

Here's what separates Elliot from Sarah: **he understood that wealth building is a math problem with a known solution.**

The formula for retiring by 40 isn't complicated:

- Live on 30% of your income, invest 70%
- Earn 10-15% average annual returns through diversified investing
- Build multiple income streams that don't require trading time for money
- Reinvest profits instead of upgrading your lifestyle

That's it. The math works every time.

But here's why most people fail: the formula is simple, but it's not easy.

WHY THIS BOOK EXISTS

Every year, millions of college graduates enter the workforce with dreams of financial success. Most will spend the next 40+ years working jobs they tolerate to pay for lifestyles they can't afford, retiring with barely enough money to survive their golden years.

A tiny percentage will make different choices. They'll sacrifice short-term comfort for long-term freedom. They'll invest in assets instead of liabilities. They'll build businesses instead of just working for businesses.

These people retire in their 30s and 40s while their peers are still decades away from financial independence.

This book is the playbook for joining that tiny percentage.

WHAT YOU'LL LEARN IN THESE PAGES

This isn't another theoretical personal finance book. This is the step-by-step story of how one person — Elliot Martinez — went from living in his parents' basement with negative net worth to achieving complete financial independence by age 40.

You'll follow Elliot's journey through:

Chapters 1-3: The Foundation

- The wake-up call that changed everything
- Breaking free from the employee mindset
- Living on 30% of your income (and loving it)

Chapters 4-6: The Building Phase

- Investing your first $100,000 in index funds
- The acceleration effect of compound interest
- Entering real estate through house flipping

Chapters 7-8: The Scaling Phase

- Building passive income through rental properties
- Commercial real estate and syndication investing
- Creating businesses that work without you

Chapters 9-10: The Independence Phase

- Optimizing your wealth machine for maximum returns
- Designing your life after financial independence
- Living the dream at 40

But this book isn't just Elliot's story — it's your blueprint. Every chapter includes specific action steps, exact strategies, and clear timelines for implementing the same wealth-building system that took Elliot from broke to financially free in 18 years.

THE TWO TYPES OF PEOPLE WHO READ THIS BOOK

Type 1: The Dreamers

These readers will love Elliot's story. They'll feel inspired by the possibilities. They'll imagine what life would be like with complete financial freedom. They might even calculate how much they'd need to save each month to retire by 40.

But they won't take action. They'll find excuses: "I don't earn enough," "I have too many expenses," "I'll start next year," "This only works for other people."

Dreamers will close this book and continue living paycheck to paycheck.

Type 2: The Doers

These readers will see Elliot's story as proof that financial independence is possible. They'll study every strategy, implement every action step, and treat this book like a manual rather than entertainment.

They'll make hard choices. They'll live below their means while their friends upgrade their lifestyles. They'll invest aggressively while others make excuses. They'll build businesses while others binge-watch Netflix.

Doers will use this book to join the small percentage of people who achieve true financial freedom.

WHICH TYPE ARE YOU?

Before you turn the page and begin Elliot's journey, you need to answer one question honestly:

Are you reading this book to be entertained by someone else's success, or are you reading it to create your own?

If you're just here for the story, you'll enjoy the next 10 chapters. Elliot's journey is inspiring and educational.

But if you're here to change your life, you need to make a commitment right now:

> **I will implement the strategies in this book.**
> **I will complete the action steps in each chapter.**
> **I will make the hard choices required to build wealth.**
> **I will not make excuses, and I will not quit when the journey becomes difficult.**

If you can make that commitment, turn the page and begin your journey to $2 million by 40.

If you can't make that commitment, put this book down and find something easier to read.

Financial independence isn't for everyone. It's only for those who want it badly enough to do what others won't.

The choice is yours.

"The best time to plant a tree was 20 years ago. The second best time is now."

Your journey to financial independence begins on the next page.

ACKNOWLEDGMENTS

This book would not exist without the people who believed in its message before it was ever written.

To my daughter, Cierra Taylor — you are the reason this book exists. Your future deserves more than the conventional path of working until 65, wondering if there's enough saved for retirement. Every page of this book was written with the hope that your generation will have the knowledge and tools to achieve true financial freedom while you're young enough to enjoy it. You gave me the drive to put these strategies on paper, and I hope one day this roadmap helps you live the life of your dreams.

To Wanda Rogers — thank you for being my muse and for helping me prove that the scenarios in this book aren't just theoretical dreams, but achievable realities. Your questions, challenges, and unwavering support pushed me to make these strategies clearer, more actionable, and more accessible. This book is better because of your influence and insight.

To every young professional who has ever felt trapped by the traditional financial advice of "work hard, save 10%, and maybe you can retire at 65" — this book is for you. Your hunger for something better inspired every chapter.

To the readers who will implement these strategies rather than just read about them — you are the ones who will prove that financial independence by 40 isn't just possible, it's inevitable when you have the right roadmap.

The path to $2 million by 40 starts now.

~ X ~

Table of Contents

THE WAKE-UP CALL 1

BREAKING FREE FROM THE EMPLOYMENT TRAP 9

THE 70/30 RULE - LIVING LIKE A STUDENT FOREVER 21

YOUR FIRST $100K - THE FOUNDATION 33

THE ACCELERATION PHASE - $100K TO $500K 47

REAL ESTATE - YOUR FIRST TASTE OF PASSIVE INCOME 59

BUILDING YOUR OWN MONEY MACHINE - STARTING A BUSINESS 75

BECOMING THE BANK - CAPITAL INVESTING 91

THE FINAL SPRINT - OPTIMIZING YOUR WEALTH MACHINE 107

LIVING THE DREAM - YOUR NEW LIFE AT 40 123

Chapter 1
THE WAKE-UP CALL

THE BASEMENT REALITY CHECK

Elliot Martinez stared at the ceiling of his childhood bedroom, the same glow-in-the-dark stars he'd stuck there in middle school now mocking him at 22. His business degree sat framed on his desk—$30,000 in student loans for a piece of paper that had landed him exactly where he started: his parents' basement.

The muffled sounds of his cousin Mike's voice drifted down from the kitchen above. Mike was 35, visiting for Sunday dinner, and Elliot could hear the familiar stress in his voice as he talked to Elliot's mom about his latest financial crisis.

"I just don't know where the money goes, Aunt Carmen," Mike was saying. "Between the mortgage, car payments, and credit cards... I'm living paycheck to paycheck. Sarah keeps talking about having kids, but how can we afford that when I can barely afford groceries?"

Elliot closed his eyes. Mike had been his role model growing up—the cool older cousin with the nice car and the good job at the marketing firm. Now Mike was a cautionary tale, trapped in what Elliot was beginning to recognize as the "normal" American financial nightmare.

His phone buzzed. A text from his college roommate Jake: "Dude, just got approved for a $25K car loan! Finally upgrading from that beater. You should see this BMW!"

Elliot felt a familiar pang of envy, followed immediately by a sinking realization. Jake was about to make the same mistake that had Mike stressed out upstairs. The same mistake that kept most people working until they were 65... or longer.

There had to be a different way.

THE COMPOUND INTEREST REVELATION

That night, unable to sleep, Elliot found himself deep in a YouTube rabbit hole about investing. One video changed everything. The presenter, a soft-spoken woman in her 40s, was explaining compound interest with a simple example:

"If you invest $500 per month starting at age 22, earning an average 10% annual return, you'll have over $2.4 million by age 40. But if you wait until age 30 to start, you'll only have about $900,000 by 40. That eight-year delay costs you over $1.5 million."

Elliot sat up in bed, his heart racing. He grabbed his laptop and started plugging numbers into a compound interest calculator. The results were staggering:

- Start at 22, invest $1,000/month: $2.4 million by 40
- Start at 25, invest $1,000/month: $1.8 million by 40
- Start at 30, invest $1,000/month: $1.1 million by 40

The message was crystal clear: time was his most valuable asset, and he was burning through it every day he delayed.

But $1,000 a month? That seemed impossible when he was living in his parents' basement with no job and $30,000 in debt.

THE MINDSET SHIFT

The next morning, Elliot cornered his dad in the garage. His father, a mechanic who'd worked for 35 years at the same shop, was organizing his tools.

"Dad, what if I told you I wanted to retire by 40?"

His father laughed, not unkindly. "Mijo, I've been working since I was 16, and I'm nowhere close to retirement at 58. That's not how the world works."

"But what if it could work differently?"

His dad paused, wrench in hand. "Look, Elliot, I've given you and your sister everything I could. But I've also watched dreams crash into reality. Focus on getting a job first, then we'll talk about dreams."

That conversation crystallized something for Elliot. His dad wasn't wrong about reality—he was wrong about what reality had to be. The traditional path—work for

40+ years, save 10% if you're lucky, retire at 65 with maybe enough to survive—wasn't the only option.

Mike's financial stress upstairs wasn't inevitable. Jake's car loan wasn't smart. There was a different game being played, and most people didn't even know it existed.

THE $2 MILLION PLAN

Over the next week, Elliot consumed everything he could find about early retirement and wealth building. He discovered the FIRE movement (Financial Independence, Retire Early), read blog after blog of people who'd done exactly what he was dreaming about.

The math was actually straightforward:

- To retire early, you need about 25 times your annual expenses saved
- If you want to spend $80,000 per year in retirement, you need $2 million
- The key was aggressive saving and smart investing
- Most importantly, you had to start NOW

The stories all had common themes: living below your means, investing aggressively, focusing on increasing income, and treating money as a tool rather than something to spend.

But they also had something else in common: they all started with someone making a decision to be different.

YOUR FINANCIAL WAKE-UP CALL

STEP 1: Calculate Your Current Net Worth

Right now, before you read another page, you need to know where you stand. Net worth is simple: everything you own minus everything you owe.

Assets (What You Own):

- Checking account balance: $_____
- Savings account balance: $_____
- Investment accounts: $_____
- Car value (realistic, not what you paid): $_____
- Other valuable items: $_____
- **Total Assets: $_____**

Liabilities (What You Owe):

- Student loans: $_____
- Credit card debt: $_____
- Car loan: $_____
- Other debts: $_____
- **Total Liabilities: $_____**

Your Net Worth = Assets - Liabilities: $_____

Don't be discouraged if this number is negative. Elliot's was -$28,500 when he started. The key is that you're starting.

STEP 2: Set Up Your Tracking System

You can't manage what you don't measure. Choose one:

Option A: Simple Spreadsheet

- Create a monthly net worth tracker
- Update it religiously on the same day each month
- Watch for the trend, not the day-to-day fluctuations

Option B: Apps and Tools

- Personal Capital (free investment tracking)
- Mint (budgeting and net worth)
- YNAB (You Need A Budget)

STEP 3: Write Down Your "Why"

This journey will be hard. There will be moments when everyone around you is spending money on things you're denying yourself. You need a compelling reason to stay the course.

Complete this sentence: **"I want to retire by 40 because..."**

Some examples:

- "I want to travel the world while I'm young and healthy"
- "I want the freedom to pursue my passion without worrying about money"
- "I want to be present for my future family without being stressed about bills"
- "I want to have choices in how I spend my time"

Write your reason down and put it somewhere you'll see it daily.

THE JOURNEY BEGINS

Elliot printed out his compound interest calculations and taped them to his bathroom mirror. Every morning, he'd see the numbers: $2.4 million by 40, but only if he started now.

The basement suddenly felt less like a failure and more like a launching pad. He had low expenses, no dependents, and most importantly, he had time — his most precious asset.

His phone buzzed. Another text from Jake: "Bro, the car payments are brutal, but it's so worth it. When are you getting something nice?"

Elliot smiled and typed back: "Working on something even better."

He wasn't just planning to get a job. He was planning to become wealthy.

But first, he needed to escape the employee mindset that kept people like Mike trapped in financial stress, and Jake trapped in debt. The traditional approach to careers — take any job, accept whatever they offer, and slowly climb the ladder — wasn't going to get him to $2 million by 40.

It was time to think differently about work itself.

In the next chapter, we'll follow Elliot as he approaches his job search not as a desperate graduate looking for any paycheck, but as a strategic wealth-builder positioning himself for maximum income growth. Because the harsh truth is this: you can't save your way to wealth if you're not earning enough to save.

Chapter 2

BREAKING FREE FROM THE EMPLOYMENT TRAP

THE DESPERATE JOB HUNT

Three weeks after his financial wake-up call, Elliot sat in the waiting room of Henderson & Associates, a mid-sized accounting firm downtown. His palms were sweaty, and his one good suit — borrowed from his dad—felt like a costume. This was his seventh interview in two weeks, and the rejections were starting to sting.

"Mr. Martinez?" A woman in her 50s appeared in the doorway. "I'm Linda, the office manager. Ready for us?"

The interview followed the same script as all the others. Tell us about yourself. Why do you want to work here? What are your salary expectations?

That last question had been tripping him up. His research showed entry-level accounting positions paid anywhere from $35,000 to $55,000, but when he'd mentioned the higher end in previous interviews, he'd seen the same polite smile that meant "thanks, but no thanks."

"I'm flexible on salary," he said this time. "I'm really just looking for an opportunity to learn and grow."

Linda nodded approvingly. "That's what we like to hear. The position starts at $32,000, with a review after six months. Does that work for you?"

Elliot's heart sank. $32,000 was barely $2,600 a month before taxes. After taxes, student loan payments, and basic living expenses, there'd be almost nothing left to invest.

But he needed a job, and he needed it now.

"That sounds great," he heard himself saying.

THE REALITY OF TRADING TIME FOR MONEY

Elliot started at Henderson & Associates on a Monday morning in March. The office was a maze of gray cubicles, flickering fluorescent lights, and the constant hum of printers and keyboards. His desk was in the corner, next to Dave, a 45-year-old staff accountant who'd been there for twelve years.

"Welcome to the machine," Dave said with a tired smile. "Coffee's in the break room, bathroom's down the hall, and your soul slowly dies somewhere around month three."

Elliot laughed nervously. "It can't be that bad."

"Kid, I make $48,000 a year. After twelve years. My rent went up $200 last month, my car needs new tires, and my daughter needs braces. You know what my raise was last year? Three percent. You know what inflation was? Four percent. I'm literally going backwards."

The first few weeks were a blur of learning the company's systems, processing invoices, and trying to make sense of tax codes. Elliot threw himself into the work, staying late, volunteering for extra projects, and studying for his CPA exam at night.

But something was nagging at him. Every morning, he'd swipe his badge at 8 AM sharp. Every evening, he'd swipe out at 5 PM (or later if there was overtime). His life was being measured in 15-minute increments, tracked by a system that saw him as a resource to be allocated.

The compound interest calculator on his phone mocked him. To hit his $2 million goal, he needed to invest $1,000 per month. His take-home pay was $2,100. After his student loan payment ($280), gas and car insurance ($200), and helping his parents with groceries ($300), he had $1,320 left. That covered his phone, some clothes, and maybe $200 toward his investment goal.

At this rate, he'd retire at 75, not 40.

THE PERFORMANCE REVIEW REALITY CHECK

Six months later, Elliot sat across from Linda for his promised review. He'd prepared a list of his accomplishments: he'd streamlined two processes, earned praise from three clients, and was ahead of schedule on his CPA exam.

"Elliot, you're doing great work," Linda began. "The partners are impressed with your dedication."

"Thank you. I was hoping we could discuss the salary adjustment you mentioned when I started."

Linda's expression shifted slightly. "Well, the budget for this year is tight. We're able to offer you a $1,500 raise, which brings you to $33,500. That's actually above average for someone at your level."

Elliot did the math in his head. $1,500 divided by 12 months was $125 per month. Before taxes, that was maybe $90 extra per month. At this rate, he'd need to work there for 20 years to get to $55,000.

"Is there a path to higher compensation?" he asked carefully.

"Of course! Dave started where you are. With dedication and time, you could be in his position in 10-12 years."

Elliot thought about Dave's warning about going backwards with inflation. "What about the senior accountant positions?"

"Those typically require CPA certification and 5-7 years of experience. They start around $65,000."

The numbers were devastating. Even if everything went perfectly—if he got his CPA, if he got promoted on schedule, if he received average raises — he'd be making $65,000 in seven years. That was $30,000 less than he needed to hit his investment goals.

THE SIDE HUSTLE REVELATION

That evening, Elliot sat in his car in the parking lot, staring at his compound interest calculator. The numbers were clear: his current path would never get him to $2 million by 40. He needed to either dramatically increase his income or dramatically decrease his timeline.

His phone rang. It was his college friend Marcus, who'd graduated with a computer science degree.

"Dude, I just picked up another freelance project," Marcus said. "This startup needs a simple website built. It's only 20 hours of work, but they're paying $3,000."

"$3,000 for 20 hours? That's $150 an hour!"

"Yeah, and that's on the low end. My main client pays me $200 an hour for backend development. I'm thinking about quitting my day job soon."

Elliot felt a familiar pang of envy, but this time it was different. Instead of just wishing he had Marcus's skills, he started thinking strategically.

"How did you learn to charge those rates?"

"It's all about positioning, man. Instead of competing with everyone else on price, I specialized in a specific type of project and became really good at it. Now I'm not just another programmer — I'm the guy who solves a specific problem better than anyone else."

After hanging up, Elliot sat in his car for another hour, thinking. The traditional employment path was a trap. You traded time for money, and someone else controlled both the time and the money. But what if there was a different way?

THE STRATEGIC CAREER PIVOT

That weekend, Elliot spent 12 hours researching high-income career paths. He studied salary surveys, job postings, and industry reports. What he discovered changed everything:

The Income Scalability Spectrum:

- **Low Scalability:** Hourly jobs, traditional employment with annual raises
- **Medium Scalability:** Sales roles, commission-based work, skilled trades
- **High Scalability:** Specialized consulting, business ownership, investment income

Most people, including his colleagues at Henderson & Associates, were stuck in the low scalability category. They were good people doing necessary work, but they were trapped in systems that limited their earning potential.

He also discovered something else: the highest-paid employees weren't necessarily the hardest workers or even the most skilled. They were the ones who understood how to position themselves as valuable, how to negotiate, and how to think strategically about their careers.

YOUR STRATEGIC CAREER ACTION PLAN

STEP 1: Identify High-Growth Industries and Roles

Don't just look for "jobs" — look for career paths with income scalability. Research these categories:

High-Growth Industries:

- Technology (software, AI, cybersecurity)
- Healthcare (specialized roles, not just general positions)
- Finance (investment banking, private equity, financial planning)
- Sales (especially B2B, software, real estate)
- Digital Marketing (performance marketing, growth hacking)
- Skilled Trades (electricians, plumbers, HVAC—but positioned as business owners)

Questions to Ask About Any Role:

- What's the income range after 5 years of experience?
- Are there commission or performance bonuses?
- Can this role lead to consulting opportunities?

- Is this a skill I could eventually use to start my own business?

STEP 2: Research Salary Ranges and Growth Potential

Use these resources:

- Glassdoor.com (salary reports by company and role)
- PayScale.com (salary ranges by experience level)
- LinkedIn (message people in target roles)
- Indeed.com (salary estimates and job postings)

Create a spreadsheet comparing:

- Starting salary
- 5-year salary potential
- Skills required
- Path to $100K+ income

STEP 3: Create Your Skills Development Plan

The highest-paid people aren't just employees — they're specialists who solve specific, valuable problems.

Identify Your Advantage:

- What are you naturally good at?
- What problems do you enjoy solving?
- What skills can you develop quickly?

- What certifications or training would dramatically increase your value?

Create a 90-Day Learning Plan:

- Choose one high-value skill to focus on
- Dedicate 1-2 hours per day to learning
- Find ways to practice this skill (even if unpaid initially)
- Document your progress and results

STEP 4: Practice Strategic Negotiation

Most people never negotiate their salary. This one skill alone can increase your lifetime earnings by hundreds of thousands of dollars.

Negotiation Principles:

- Never accept the first offer
- Always negotiate based on value, not need
- Research market rates thoroughly
- Practice your pitch out loud
- Be prepared to walk away

Practice Scenarios:

- Initial job offer negotiation
- Annual review conversations
- Asking for additional responsibilities

- Requesting professional development opportunities

THE AWAKENING

On Monday morning, Elliot walked into Henderson & Associates with a new perspective. He wasn't just an employee anymore—he was a strategic player in his own wealth-building game.

During his lunch break, he updated his LinkedIn profile and started researching financial planning roles. The top financial advisors weren't just earning $100K+—they were earning $300K, $500K, or more. They were building businesses, not just working jobs.

Dave noticed the change immediately. "You seem different today. Everything okay?"

"Actually, yeah. I think I'm finally starting to understand how this all works."

"How what works?"

"The game. I've been playing it wrong."

Dave looked confused, but Elliot just smiled. He was beginning to realize that his time at Henderson & Associates wasn't a career — it was graduate school. He was learning valuable skills, building his resume, and most importantly, he was learning exactly what he didn't want his future to look like.

His phone buzzed with a text from Marcus: "Just signed a $15K project. Three months of work, all remote. This freelance thing is crazy."

Elliot typed back: "Tell me more. I think I'm ready to learn."

As he hit send, he realized he was no longer just dreaming about retiring by 40. He was planning for it. And the first step was breaking free from the employee mindset that kept people like Dave trapped in financial mediocrity.

The traditional path—trade time for money, accept whatever raise they give you, and hope for the best—wasn't going to get him to $2 million. But now he was starting to see the alternative.

In our next chapter, we'll follow Elliot as he faces his biggest challenge yet: learning to live like a student while earning a real salary. Because no matter how much he increases his income, he'll never build wealth if he falls into the lifestyle inflation trap that captures most young professionals.

Chapter 3

THE 70/30 RULE - LIVING LIKE A STUDENT FOREVER

THE TEMPTATION TRAP

Eight months into his job at Henderson & Associates, Elliot faced his first real test. His tax refund had come in—$1,800—and his cousin Mike was getting married. The bachelor party was in Vegas, and everyone was staying at the Bellagio.

"Come on, man," his friend Jake texted. "It's only $800 for the weekend. You're working now, you can afford it."

Elliot stared at his phone, torn. He'd been living in his parents' basement for almost a year, driving his dad's old Honda, and wearing the same rotation of five work shirts. His coworkers had started inviting him to happy hours, but he always declined. "I'm saving for something big," he'd say, but even he was starting to doubt himself.

His investment account showed a pathetic $1,200. At this rate, he'd need 150 years to reach $2 million.

The Vegas trip represented everything he'd been denying himself. His friends were living it up, buying new cars, getting their own apartments, dating. Meanwhile, he was eating ramen and studying compound interest calculators like they were religious texts.

"What's the point of making money if you never spend it?" Jake had asked him the week before.

That question haunted him as he sat in his childhood bedroom, staring at the bachelor party group chat. Photos of his friends' new apartments, their weekend trips, their restaurant dinners. They all seemed so... normal. So happy.

Maybe he was taking this early retirement thing too seriously.

THE MOMENT OF TRUTH

The next morning, Elliot found himself in the kitchen with his mom, who was making breakfast before her shift at the hospital.

"Mijo, you've seemed stressed lately. Everything okay with work?"

"Work's fine, Mom. It's just... I don't know. Sometimes I wonder if I'm missing out on being young."

His mother sat down across from him, her scrubs still smelling like hospital disinfectant. "You know, when your father and I were your age, we thought we had plenty of time to save money. We'd do it later, when we made more, when things settled down."

"But you guys did fine."

"Did we?" She smiled sadly. "Your father's 58, and his back is shot from working in that garage. We have maybe $30,000 saved for retirement. If it weren't for his pension — which might not even exist when he retires— we'd be in real trouble."

She reached across and squeezed his hand. "I see you making different choices, and I'm proud of you. But I also see you struggling with those choices. That's normal."

"How do you know you're making the right decision when everyone else thinks you're crazy?"

"You don't. But you look at where the 'normal' choices lead people, and you decide if that's what you want."

Elliot thought about Dave at work, stressed about his daughter's braces. About Mike, living paycheck to paycheck at 35. About his parents, working into their 60s because they had no choice.

He texted Jake back: "Can't make Vegas, but have an amazing time. Send photos!"

Jake's response came immediately: "Dude, you're becoming weird. It's $800, not $8,000."

But Elliot had done the math. $800 invested at 22, earning 10% annually, would be worth $13,500 by the time he turned 40. That weekend in Vegas would cost him $13,500 in future wealth.

THE 70/30 REVELATION

That weekend, instead of Vegas, Elliot spent Saturday morning at the library reading personal finance books. One book changed everything: "Your Money or Your Life" by Vicki Robin.

The concept was simple but revolutionary: every dollar you spend represents hours of your life you traded to earn that dollar. When you buy something, you're not just spending money — you're spending your life energy.

But the book went deeper. It introduced him to the concept of the savings rate—the percentage of your income that you save and invest. Most Americans saved 5-10% of their income. The early retirement community saved 50-70%.

The math was brutal but clear:

- Save 10% of income: 51 years to retirement
- Save 25% of income: 32 years to retirement
- Save 50% of income: 17 years to retirement
- Save 70% of income: 8.5 years to retirement

If Elliot could live on 30% of his income and save 70%, he could retire in less than 10 years, not 40.

But living on 30% of his income meant living on about $1,000 per month. That was less than most people spent on rent alone.

THE STUDENT LIFESTYLE STRATEGY

Elliot pulled out a notebook and started calculating. His current expenses:

- Living at home: $300 (helping parents)
- Car insurance: $120/month
- Gas: $80/month
- Food: $400/month
- Phone: $80/month
- Clothes/miscellaneous: $200/month
- Student loan minimum: $280/month
- **Total: $1,460/month**

His take-home pay was $2,100. If he could get his expenses down to $1,000, he could save $1,100 per month. That was close to his goal.

But cutting $460 from his budget meant making some serious changes.

Food: $400 → $200
This was his biggest expense after rent. He'd been eating lunch out most days ($12-15), grabbing coffee ($5), and buying groceries without planning ($80-100/week).

Clothes/Miscellaneous: $200 → $50
He'd been buying new clothes to "look professional" and spending money on small things that added up.

Everything from movie tickets to apps to "just a quick stop" at Target.

Phone: $80 → $40
He was paying for unlimited data he barely used. A basic plan would cut this in half.

The plan was aggressive, but it was possible. More importantly, it was temporary. Once his income increased, he could maintain the same lifestyle while his savings rate exploded.

THE PSYCHOLOGICAL BATTLE

The first month was brutal. Elliot meal-prepped every Sunday, making large batches of rice, beans, and chicken that he'd eat all week. He brought coffee from home in a thermos. He declined every social invitation that cost money.

His friends started to worry about him.

"Are you okay financially?" his college friend Sarah asked. "You haven't been out with us in weeks."

"I'm fine. Just focusing on some goals."

"What goals could be more important than living your life?"

How could he explain that he was trying to buy his life back? That every dollar he didn't spend today was a dollar that would work for him for the next 18 years?

The worst part was the judgment. His coworkers thought he was cheap. His friends thought he was becoming antisocial. Even his family worried he was taking things too far.

"You're young," his aunt said at a family gathering. "You should be enjoying yourself, not living like a monk."

But Elliot had started to see something his critics couldn't: the hidden cost of "enjoying yourself."

Jake's Instagram was full of photos from Vegas, but Elliot had done the math. Jake had spent $800 on the weekend, plus $200 for new clothes, plus $150 for drinks throughout the month. That was $1,150—more than Elliot's entire monthly budget.

Meanwhile, Elliot's investment account was growing. $1,200 became $2,400. Then $3,800. For the first time in his life, he was watching his money multiply instead of disappear.

THE COMPOUND EFFECT

By month three of his aggressive savings plan, something unexpected happened. Elliot stopped missing the things he'd given up.

Cooking at home had become a relaxing routine. He'd discovered he actually enjoyed meal prep, and he was eating healthier than he ever had. The coffee shop visits had been mindless habit, not genuine pleasure.

More importantly, he'd started to see his friends' spending differently. They weren't enjoying their money — they were using it to fill time, to avoid boredom, to feel better about jobs they didn't love.

"I bought this watch to celebrate my promotion," Dave at work said, showing off a $300 timepiece. "I deserve it after all that overtime."

But Elliot saw something else: Dave was celebrating a 3% raise with a purchase that represented 10% of his annual raise. He was spending his progress before he'd even received it.

The mental shift was profound. Instead of feeling deprived, Elliot started feeling empowered. Every dollar he didn't spend was a dollar working toward his freedom.

YOUR 70/30 ACTION PLAN

STEP 1: Calculate Your Current Expenses

Before you can optimize, you need to know where your money goes. Track every expense for one month. Don't change your spending — just record it.

Categories to Track:

- Housing (rent/mortgage, utilities, insurance)
- Transportation (car payment, gas, insurance, maintenance)

- Food (groceries, restaurants, coffee, bars)
- Entertainment (movies, streaming, hobbies)
- Shopping (clothes, electronics, miscellaneous)
- Debt payments (student loans, credit cards)
- Insurance (health, dental, vision)
- Subscriptions (gym, apps, services)

Your Monthly Total: $_____

STEP 2: Identify Your "Big Three" Expenses

For most people, 70% of expenses fall into three categories:

1. Housing
2. Transportation
3. Food

These are where you'll find the biggest savings opportunities.

Housing Optimization:

- Live with roommates or family longer than you planned
- Choose location based on total cost (rent + transportation)
- Consider house hacking (rent out rooms)
- Avoid luxury amenities you don't actually use

Transportation Optimization:

- Keep your current car as long as possible
- Buy used cars in cash when you must upgrade
- Live close to work to reduce commuting costs
- Consider biking or public transit

Food Optimization:

- Cook 80% of meals at home
- Meal prep on weekends
- Buy generic brands
- Limit restaurant visits to special occasions

STEP 3: Create Your 70/30 Budget

Take your monthly take-home pay and multiply by 0.30. This is your new spending limit.

Monthly Take-Home Pay: $_____
30% Spending Limit: $_____
70% Savings Goal: $_____

Now allocate your 30% spending budget:

- Housing: 40% of spending limit
- Transportation: 25% of spending limit
- Food: 20% of spending limit
- Everything else: 15% of spending limit

STEP 4: Automate Your Savings

Set up automatic transfers on payday:

- 70% to investment accounts
- 30% to checking for expenses

This removes the temptation to spend money that should be invested.

Recommended Account Structure:

- Checking: Monthly expenses only
- Emergency fund: 3-6 months of expenses
- Investment account: Everything else

THE BREAKTHROUGH MONTH

Six months into his 70/30 plan, Elliot hit his first major milestone: $10,000 in investments. It had taken him 23 years to save his first $1,000, and only 6 months to get from $1,000 to $10,000.

More importantly, he'd proven to himself that extreme saving was possible. He wasn't just surviving on 30% of his income—he was thriving.

His coworkers had stopped commenting on his lunch routine. His friends had stopped inviting him to expensive activities, but the ones who truly cared had started suggesting free alternatives. Movie nights at home instead of theaters. Hiking instead of expensive dinners.

The lifestyle had become sustainable, even enjoyable.

But Elliot was starting to realize something else: saving 70% of a $33,500 salary was impressive, but it would still take him 15+ years to reach $2 million. The 70/30 rule had taught him to live below his means, but if he really wanted to retire by 40, he needed to dramatically increase his means.

His phone buzzed with a text from Marcus: "Just landed a $200/hour consulting gig. Working 20 hours a week from home. This is insane."

Elliot smiled. He'd mastered the art of living on almost nothing. Now it was time to master the art of earning significantly more.

The student lifestyle had been phase one. Phase two was about to begin.

In our next chapter, we'll follow Elliot as he combines his newfound savings discipline with strategic income growth, learning how to invest his first $100,000 — the hardest but most crucial milestone on the path to wealth.

Chapter 4

YOUR FIRST $100K - THE FOUNDATION

THE PARALYSIS OF CHOICE

Elliot stared at his laptop screen, overwhelmed. His investment account had grown to $18,000 over the past ten months — a number that would have seemed impossible when he started. But now he faced a new problem: analysis paralysis.

His money was sitting in a basic savings account earning 0.5% interest while inflation ate away at its purchasing power. He'd been researching investments for weeks, but every article seemed to contradict the last one.

"Buy index funds," said one blog. "Individual stocks are the way to build real wealth," argued another. "Real estate is the only true hedge against inflation," claimed a third.

His coworker Dave had noticed him reading financial websites during lunch breaks. "You're young," Dave had said. "Just put it all in tech stocks. Apple, Google, Microsoft — they can't go wrong."

But Elliot's college friend Sarah had lost $5,000 day-trading crypto the previous year. "I thought I was smart," she'd told him. "Turns out the market is smarter than all of us."

The more he researched, the more confused he became. Options, futures, bonds, REITs, growth stocks, value stocks, small-cap, large-cap—the terminology alone was overwhelming.

Meanwhile, his $18,000 was losing value every day it sat in savings.

THE MENTOR APPEARS

The breakthrough came from an unexpected source. Elliot had been working late on a complex tax return when he overheard a conversation between two of the firm's clients in the waiting room.

"The thing about investing," one was saying, "is that time in the market beats timing the market. I've been putting the same amount into index funds every month for twenty years. Never tried to pick individual stocks, never tried to time the market. Just consistent investing."

"How's that worked out?" the other asked.

"My portfolio's worth about $800,000 now. Started with $500 a month."

Elliot's ears perked up. After the clients left, he looked up their files. The first man, Robert Chen, was a 48-year-old engineer who'd been the firm's client for five years. His tax returns showed exactly what he'd described —

steady, consistent investment contributions and substantial investment income.

The next day, Elliot worked up the courage to call Robert's office.

"Mr. Chen? This is Elliot Martinez from Henderson & Associates. I hope you don't mind me calling, but I overheard your conversation yesterday about investing, and I wondered if you might be willing to share some advice with someone just starting out."

Robert chuckled. "You're the young guy who's been staying late, right? Linda mentioned you were working hard. Sure, I'd be happy to chat. How about coffee this Saturday?"

THE $100K LESSON

That Saturday morning at a small café downtown, Robert shared the most important investment lesson Elliot would ever learn.

"The first $100,000 is the hardest," Robert said, stirring his coffee. "Not because the investing is complicated, but because it requires the most discipline and patience. After that, compound interest starts doing the heavy lifting."

He pulled out his phone and showed Elliot a compound interest calculator. "Look at this. If you invest $1,000 a month earning 10% annually, it takes you about 7 years to reach your first $100,000. But it only takes 4 more years to reach your second $100,000. And then 3 years to reach your third."

The math was staggering:

- Years 1-7: $0 to $100,000
- Years 8-11: $100,000 to $200,000
- Years 12-14: $200,000 to $300,000
- Years 15-17: $300,000 to $400,000

"The first $100K is like pushing a boulder uphill," Robert continued. "You're doing most of the work. After that, gravity starts helping you, and the boulder rolls faster and faster."

"But how do I know I'm investing in the right things?"

Robert smiled. "That's the beautiful thing about index funds. You don't have to know. You just have to know that the overall market, over long periods, goes up."

THE SIMPLE STRATEGY

Over the next hour, Robert laid out the investment strategy that would change Elliot's life:

The Three-Fund Portfolio:

1. **Total Stock Market Index (70%):** Owns a piece of every publicly traded company in America
2. **International Stock Index (20%):** Diversifies across global markets

3. **Bond Index (10%):** Provides stability and income

"That's it?" Elliot asked. "No picking individual stocks? No trying to time the market?"

"Nope. The smartest investors in the world can't consistently beat the market. But they can match it, and matching the market over 20+ years makes you wealthy."

Robert showed him the historical data. Over any 20-year period since 1926, the stock market had never lost money. The average annual return was about 10%, though individual years varied wildly.

"Some years you'll lose 30%," Robert warned. "Some years you'll gain 30%. The key is to keep investing through both. Dollar-cost averaging smooths out the volatility."

Dollar-Cost Averaging: Investing the same amount every month regardless of market conditions. When prices are high, you buy fewer shares. When prices are low, you buy more shares. Over time, you average out the price fluctuations.

"What about picking individual stocks?"

"Do you want to spend your time researching companies, reading financial statements, and trying to outsmart professional fund managers? Or do you want to let the market work for you while you focus on increasing your income?"

The choice was obvious.

THE FIRST INVESTMENT

Monday morning, Elliot opened accounts with Vanguard, the company Robert recommended for low-cost index funds. The website was simpler than he'd expected:

- **Vanguard Total Stock Market Index Fund (VTSAX):** 0.03% expense ratio

- **Vanguard Total International Stock Index Fund (VTIAX):** 0.11% expense ratio

- **Vanguard Total Bond Market Index Fund (VBTLX):** 0.05% expense ratio

The expense ratios were tiny—for every $10,000 invested, he'd pay just $3-11 in annual fees. Compare that to actively managed funds that charged 1-2% annually.

His allocation:

- 70% VTSAX ($12,600)

- 20% VTIAX ($3,600)

- 10% VBTLX ($1,800)

With shaking hands, Elliot transferred his $18,000 from savings and made his first investment. The confirmation screen showed he now owned 0.000001% of Apple, Google, Microsoft, and thousands of other companies.

It was terrifying and exhilarating at the same time.

THE ROLLER COASTER BEGINS

Elliot's first month as an investor was a baptism by fire. The market dropped 8% in the first two weeks, turning his $18,000 into $16,560. He'd lost $1,440 in two weeks—more than he'd saved in his first three months of working.

His first instinct was to sell everything and cut his losses. He called Robert in a panic.

"This is normal," Robert said calmly. "The market has downturns. The question is: has anything changed about your long-term investment thesis?"

"What do you mean?"

"Do you still believe that American businesses will be worth more in 20 years than they are today? Do you still believe that innovation, productivity, and human ingenuity will drive economic growth?"

"Yes, but—"

"Then this is just noise. In fact, it's an opportunity. Your $1,000 monthly investment will buy more shares this month than it did last month."

Robert was right. When Elliot made his second monthly investment, his $1,000 bought more shares because prices were lower. He was getting the same companies at a discount.

By the end of the month, the market had recovered, and his account was back to $18,200. Plus his new $1,000 investment.

The lesson was profound: short-term volatility was the price you paid for long-term returns.

THE AUTOMATION SYSTEM

Three months into his investing journey, Elliot had refined his system:

Automatic Investing Schedule:

- 1st of month: $700 to VTSAX
- 1st of month: $200 to VTIAX
- 1st of month: $100 to VBTLX

Account Structure:

- Checking: Monthly expenses only ($1,000)
- Emergency fund: $6,000 (6 months of expenses)
- Investment account: Everything else

Rules:

1. Never check account balances daily (too emotional)
2. Check monthly only to rebalance if needed
3. Increase contributions with every raise
4. Never time the market or pick individual stocks

The automation removed emotion from the equation. Whether the market was up or down, his investments continued like clockwork.

YOUR FIRST $100K ACTION PLAN

STEP 1: Choose Your Investment Platform

Look for platforms with:

- Low expense ratios (under 0.2% for index funds)
- No transaction fees for index funds
- Easy automatic investing
- Strong reputation and stability

Recommended Platforms:

- **Vanguard** (lowest costs, excellent index funds)
- **Fidelity** (competitive costs, good customer service)
- **Charles Schwab** (strong platform, good mobile app)

STEP 2: Open Your Investment Accounts

Tax-Advantaged Accounts (Open These First):

- **401(k):** Employer-sponsored, often with matching
- **IRA:** Individual Retirement Account, $6,000 annual limit

- **Roth IRA:** After-tax contributions, tax-free growth

Taxable Investment Account:

- For investments beyond retirement account limits
- More flexibility but less tax efficiency

STEP 3: Choose Your Investment Allocation

Simple Three-Fund Portfolio:

- Age 20-30: 80% stocks, 20% bonds
- Age 30-40: 70% stocks, 30% bonds
- Age 40-50: 60% stocks, 40% bonds

Within Your Stock Allocation:

- 70% US Total Market Index
- 30% International Index

Sample Allocation for 25-Year-Old:

- 56% US Total Market Index (70% of 80%)
- 24% International Index (30% of 80%)
- 20% Bond Index

STEP 4: Automate Your Investing

Set up automatic transfers:

- From checking to investment account
- From investment account to specific funds

- Increase contributions with every raise

Monthly Investment Schedule:
- Same day each month (avoid market timing)
- Same dollar amount (dollar-cost averaging)
- Rebalance quarterly if allocation drifts more than 5%

THE $50K MILESTONE

Eighteen months after his first investment, Elliot hit $50,000 in his investment accounts. The milestone came faster than expected because he'd received two raises and consistently increased his contributions.

His monthly investment had grown from $1,000 to $1,400, and he'd added his tax refund and a small bonus to his accounts.

More importantly, he'd survived his first major market correction. In month 14, the market dropped 15% over six weeks. This time, instead of panicking, Elliot had increased his contributions, buying more shares at lower prices.

"You're becoming a real investor," Robert told him over their quarterly coffee meeting. "The hardest part is behind you."

"What do you mean?"

"You've learned to ignore the noise. You've automated your system. You've survived your first major downturn. Now it's just a matter of staying consistent and letting compound interest do its work."

Elliot looked at his compound interest calculator. At his current contribution rate, he'd hit $100,000 in about 30 more months. His second $100,000 would take only 18 months after that.

The boulder was starting to roll.

But Robert had also mentioned something else that intrigued him: "Your next challenge won't be investing—it'll be increasing your income fast enough to feed your investment machine."

Elliot's salary had grown from $32,000 to $42,000, but he was starting to realize that traditional employment, even with regular raises, wouldn't get him to $2 million by 40. He needed to think bigger.

His phone buzzed with a text from Marcus: "Just bought my first rental property. Cash flow positive from day one. Real estate is wild."

Elliot smiled. His investment foundation was solid, but maybe it was time to explore other wealth-building vehicles.

In our next chapter, we'll follow Elliot as he discovers the power of real estate investing, learns about leverage and passive income, and begins building his first alternative income stream outside of traditional employment.

Chapter 5

THE ACCELERATION PHASE - $100K TO $500K

THE MAGIC NUMBER

Elliot stared at his phone screen in disbelief. His investment account had just crossed $100,000 for the first time. After taxes and fees, the number read $100,247.

He was 25 years old and worth more than his parents had saved in their entire lives.

The milestone had come faster than his original projections. What he'd thought would take seven years had taken just under four, thanks to aggressive saving, consistent raises, and a strong market run. More importantly, he could see the compound interest acceleration that Robert had promised.

His latest monthly statement told the story:

- Monthly contributions: $1,800
- Investment gains: $2,100
- Total monthly increase: $3,900

For the first time, his money was working harder than he was. His investments had earned more in one month than he used to make in two months at his first job.

But the celebration was tempered by a sobering realization: at his current pace, he'd reach $500,000 in about six more years, putting him at age 31. That would leave only nine years to accumulate the remaining $1.5 million to reach his goal by 40.

The math was getting tight.

THE INCOME BREAKTHROUGH

The answer came during his annual performance review at Henderson & Associates. Elliot had been promoted to Senior Tax Associate with a salary bump to $58,000 — a significant increase, but still not enough to dramatically accelerate his timeline.

During the review, his manager Linda mentioned something that changed everything.

"Elliot, you've become our go-to person for complex tax situations. Some of our clients have specifically requested to work with you. Have you ever considered tax consulting on the side?"

"Is that allowed?"

"As long as it doesn't compete with our services directly, yes. In fact, several of our staff do freelance work. There's a huge demand for qualified tax preparers who can handle complex situations."

That weekend, Elliot researched the freelance tax preparation market. What he discovered was a goldmine:

- Experienced CPAs charged $150-300 per hour for consulting
- Tax preparation for small businesses: $500-2,000 per return
- Wealthy individuals paid $200-500 per hour for tax planning
- The work was seasonal, concentrated in January through April

But there was a catch: he needed his CPA license to command top rates.

THE SIDE HUSTLE STRATEGY

Elliot threw himself into CPA exam preparation with the same intensity he'd brought to saving money. He studied two hours every morning before work and four hours on weekends. The material was challenging, but he had a powerful motivator: every hour of study was an investment in dramatically higher earning potential.

Six months later, he passed all four sections of the CPA exam on his first attempt.

Armed with his new credentials, Elliot launched "Martinez Tax Solutions" in January. His strategy was simple:

- Target small business owners who needed more sophisticated help than basic tax software
- Offer competitive rates ($125/hour) to build a client base
- Provide exceptional service to generate referrals
- Work evenings and weekends to avoid conflicts with his day job

His first client came through a referral from Robert Chen. A small restaurant owner needed help with payroll tax issues and quarterly filings. The project took 12 hours at $125/hour — $1,500 for weekend work.

"This is what I've been missing," Elliot realized. Instead of trading his time for a fixed salary, he was trading his expertise for premium rates.

THE MULTIPLICATION EFFECT

By the end of his first tax season, Elliot had earned $18,000 from his side practice—more than half his annual salary at Henderson & Associates. But more importantly, he'd learned something crucial about income scalability.

His day job paid him $58,000 regardless of how much value he created. Whether he processed 100 tax returns or 500, his paycheck remained the same. But his consulting practice paid him directly for value creation. The more problems he solved, the more he earned.

The psychological shift was profound. At his day job, he was an expense on someone else's profit and loss statement. In his consulting practice, he was the profit.

His friend Marcus noticed the change immediately. "You seem different, man. More confident."

"I think I'm finally understanding how money really works," Elliot replied.

"What do you mean?"

"Most people think you get rich by working harder. But you actually get rich by working smarter — creating more value per hour of your time."

THE INVESTMENT ACCELERATION

The extra $18,000 from consulting went straight into his investment accounts, pushing his monthly investment contributions to $3,300. Combined with his day job savings, he was now investing over $40,000 per year.

The acceleration was dramatic:

- Age 22-25: $0 to $100,000 (4 years)
- Age 25-26: $100,000 to $140,000 (1 year)
- Projected age 26-28: $140,000 to $300,000 (2 years)

But Elliot was learning that diversification applied to more than just his investment portfolio—it applied to his income streams too.

His mentor Robert had multiple income sources:

- Engineering salary: $120,000
- Patent royalties: $30,000 annually
- Investment dividends: $45,000 annually
- Real estate rental income: $24,000 annually

"The wealthy never depend on just one income source," Robert explained during one of their coffee meetings. "They build systems that generate money even when they're not actively working."

THE TAX OPTIMIZATION STRATEGY

As Elliot's income and investments grew, taxes became a bigger concern. His CPA knowledge was paying dividends beyond just his consulting income—he was learning to legally minimize his tax burden.

Key Strategies He Implemented:

Business Expense Deductions:

- Home office for consulting practice
- Professional development and education
- Business equipment and software
- Mileage for client meetings

Tax-Advantaged Account Maximization:

- Maxed out 401(k): $22,500 annually
- Maxed out IRA: $6,000 annually

- Opened SEP-IRA for consulting income: Additional $14,500

Strategic Tax Loss Harvesting:

- Sold losing investments to offset gains
- Immediately reinvested in similar but not identical funds
- Avoided wash sale rules while maintaining market exposure

The tax savings added up to thousands of dollars annually—money that went straight into investments.

THE SKILL INVESTMENT PHILOSOPHY

Elliot's success with the CPA certification taught him a crucial lesson: the highest ROI investments weren't always financial—sometimes they were educational.

He calculated the return on his CPA investment:

- Cost: $3,000 (study materials, exam fees, time)
- Additional annual income: $20,000+ (and growing)
- ROI: 667% in the first year alone

This led to his "skill investment" philosophy: continuously developing capabilities that commanded premium market rates.

His next targets:

- Financial planning certification (CFP)
- Real estate license
- Investment advisor credentials

Each certification would open new income opportunities and deepen his understanding of wealth building.

YOUR ACCELERATION ACTION PLAN

STEP 1: Identify Your Income Scalability Opportunities

Assess Your Current Role:

- Can you earn more by working more hours? (Limited scalability)
- Can you earn more by creating more value? (Medium scalability)
- Can you earn money without trading time? (High scalability)

High-Scalability Career Moves:

- Sales roles with uncapped commissions
- Consulting in your area of expertise
- Professional certifications that command premium rates

- Building expertise in high-demand, low-supply skills

STEP 2: Develop Premium Skills

Identify High-Value Skills in Your Industry:

- What do the top 10% earners in your field know that others don't?
- What certifications or credentials unlock higher compensation?
- What emerging skills will be valuable in 3-5 years?

Create Your Skill Development Plan:

- Choose one high-impact skill to develop
- Set aside 10 hours per week for learning
- Find mentors who've successfully monetized these skills
- Practice with real projects, even if unpaid initially

STEP 3: Launch Your Side Income Stream

Consulting/Freelancing Strategy:

- Start with competitive rates to build client base
- Deliver exceptional value to generate referrals
- Gradually raise rates as demand increases
- Systematize processes to increase efficiency

Client Acquisition Methods:

- Leverage your existing network
- Ask for referrals from satisfied clients
- Use your day job connections (where appropriate)
- Build a simple website showcasing your expertise

STEP 4: Maximize Tax-Advantaged Investing

Priority Order:

1. 401(k) match (free money)
2. Max 401(k) contribution ($22,500)
3. Max IRA contribution ($6,000)
4. SEP-IRA or Solo 401(k) for side business income
5. Taxable investment accounts

Advanced Tax Strategies:

- Tax loss harvesting in taxable accounts
- Asset location (bonds in tax-advantaged, stocks in taxable)
- Backdoor Roth IRA if income limits apply
- Business expense optimization

THE $250K MILESTONE

Two years after hitting $100,000, Elliot's net worth crossed $250,000. The acceleration was exactly what Robert had predicted—each milestone came faster than the last.

His income sources had diversified:

- Day job salary: $65,000 (after another promotion)
- Tax consulting: $35,000 annually
- Investment gains: $28,000 (in a good market year)
- Total annual income: $128,000

More importantly, his investment contributions had grown from $1,000 per month to $4,500 per month. He was investing more each month than he used to earn in two months.

But Elliot was starting to see the limits of his current strategy. Even with aggressive saving and strong market returns, reaching $2 million by 40 would require something more than just stock market investing.

His consulting clients had been asking him about real estate investments, and several mentioned the tax advantages and passive income potential. Marcus had been sending him photos of his growing rental property portfolio, showing monthly cash flow statements that were impressive.

"You should look into real estate," Robert mentioned during their latest coffee meeting. "I wish I'd started earlier. The combination of cash flow, appreciation, and tax benefits is powerful."

Elliot pulled up his compound interest calculator one more time. To reach $2 million by 40, he needed to accelerate his wealth building beyond traditional investments.

It was time to explore leverage, passive income, and real estate.

His phone buzzed with a text from Marcus: "Just closed on property #3. Monthly cash flow is now $2,400. Real estate is the cheat code for building wealth."

Elliot smiled. Phase two of his wealth building was about to begin.

In our next chapter, we'll follow Elliot as he takes his first steps into real estate investing, learning about leverage, cash flow, and passive income while navigating the challenges of becoming a landlord.

Chapter 6

REAL ESTATE - YOUR FIRST TASTE OF PASSIVE INCOME

THE EYE-OPENING CONVERSATION

Elliot sat in Marcus's garage, watching his friend sand down kitchen cabinets that would soon be installed in a house across town. Marcus had invited him over to see his latest project—a single-family home he'd bought for $85,000, was renovating, and planned to sell for $140,000.

"So you're telling me you'll make $55,000 profit in four months?" Elliot asked, trying to wrap his head around the numbers.

Marcus paused his sanding and wiped his hands on a rag. "Well, not pure profit. I've got about $20,000 in renovation costs, plus holding costs, realtor fees, and taxes. But yeah, I should clear about $30,000 when it's all said and done."

"That's more than I make in half a year at my day job."

"And this is just my third flip. The first one I barely broke even because I didn't know what I was doing. The second one netted me $18,000. I'm getting better at estimating costs and finding the right properties."

Elliot walked through the house with Marcus, noting the strategic improvements: fresh paint, new flooring, updated kitchen, modern light fixtures. Nothing fancy, but everything clean and move-in ready.

"The key," Marcus explained, "is buying in neighborhoods where people want to live but finding houses that need cosmetic work, not structural repairs. Most buyers can't see past ugly carpet and outdated paint."

"How do you know what to fix and what to leave alone?"

"Experience, mostly. But also understanding your buyer. This neighborhood attracts first-time homebuyers and young families. They want something that looks good in photos and doesn't need immediate work, but they're not expecting luxury finishes."

THE LEARNING PHASE

That night, Elliot couldn't stop thinking about what he'd seen. While his stock investments were growing steadily, they were passive. Real estate offered something different—the opportunity to create value through his own efforts and decisions.

He spent the next month immersing himself in real estate education:

Books:

- "FLIP: How to Find, Fix, and Sell Houses for Profit" by Rick Villani

- "The Book on Flipping Houses" by J. Scott
- "Real Estate Flipping Bible" by Wayne Turner

YouTube Channels:

- Tarek and Christina El Moussa (Flip or Flop)
- BiggerPockets House Flipping videos
- Local contractors showing renovation techniques

Local Resources:

- Home Depot weekend workshops
- Local real estate investment meetup groups
- Conversations with contractors about costs and timelines

What he learned was both exciting and sobering:

The Potential:

- Significant profits possible in 3-6 months
- Ability to use leverage (hard money loans) to do deals with less cash
- Hands-on control over the investment outcome
- Skills that transferred to all real estate investing

The Risks:

- Cost overruns could eliminate profits quickly
- Market changes during renovation period

- Permit issues and code violations
- Contractor delays and quality problems
- Competition from experienced flippers

The Reality Check:

- Most beginners underestimated costs by 20-50%
- Successful flipping required construction knowledge or reliable contractors
- It was a business, not a passive investment
- Timing was crucial — holding costs added up quickly

MARKET ANALYSIS AND STRATEGY

Elliot decided to approach house flipping like he'd approached stock investing—with systematic research and conservative assumptions.

He spent weekends driving through neighborhoods, analyzing recent sales and current listings. He created a spreadsheet tracking:

- Recent sales by neighborhood
- Average days on market
- Price per square foot trends
- Types of properties that sold quickly
- Common renovation needs

His target criteria emerged:

- 3-bedroom, 2-bathroom houses (highest demand)
- Built 1970-1990 (avoiding major structural issues)
- 1,200-1,500 square feet (manageable renovation scope)
- Purchase price under $100,000
- In neighborhoods where renovated homes sold for $130,000+

After analyzing 200+ properties over two months, Elliot identified his target area: Riverside Heights, a working-class neighborhood near downtown where young professionals were starting to buy.

THE FIRST DEAL

The property that changed everything was a 1978 ranch house listed for $89,000. The photos showed brown carpet, wood paneling, and a kitchen from the Carter administration. But the bones were good—solid foundation, newer roof, and a layout that worked.

Property Details:

- 3 bedrooms, 2 bathrooms, 1,350 square feet
- Last updated in 1985
- Motivated seller (estate sale)

- Comparable sales: $135,000-145,000 for renovated homes

Elliot walked through the house with a contractor Marcus had recommended. Together, they created a renovation budget:

Renovation Cost Estimate:

- Flooring (laminate throughout): $4,500
- Paint (interior and exterior): $3,000
- Kitchen cabinets and countertops: $8,000
- Bathroom updates: $4,000
- Light fixtures and hardware: $1,500
- Landscaping and curb appeal: $2,000
- **Total estimated costs: $23,000**

Deal Analysis:

- Purchase price: $89,000
- Renovation costs: $23,000
- Holding costs (6 months): $4,000
- Selling costs (6% realtor + closing): $9,000
- **Total investment: $125,000**
- **Expected sale price: $140,000**
- **Projected profit: $15,000**

The numbers worked, but barely. There was little room for error.

FINANCING THE DEAL

Unlike his stock investments, the house flip required significant upfront capital. Elliot had several options:

Traditional Mortgage: 20% down plus renovation costs

- Required: $18,000 down + $23,000 renovation = $41,000 cash
- Timeline: 30-45 days to close
- Interest rate: 5.5%

Hard Money Loan: 70% of purchase price plus renovation

- Required: $27,000 down payment + $6,000 in renovation costs = $33,000 cash
- Timeline: 7-10 days to close
- Interest rate: 12% plus 2 points

Cash Purchase: Use investment funds directly

- Required: $112,000 total ($89,000 + $23,000)
- Timeline: 7 days to close
- Interest cost: Opportunity cost of not having money in stock market

After running the numbers, Elliot chose the hard money route. It required less cash upfront and allowed him to keep more of his investment portfolio intact.

THE RENOVATION REALITY

Closing on his first flip was terrifying and exhilarating. Standing in the empty house with the keys in his hand, Elliot realized he'd just committed $33,000 and the next four months of his life to a project he'd never done before.

The renovation started smoothly. Demo went fast—removing carpet, tearing out old cabinets, and scraping wallpaper. But by week three, reality set in:

Week 3: Electrician discovered outdated wiring that needed updating

- Unexpected cost: $2,800
- Timeline delay: 1 week

Week 5: Plumber found water damage behind kitchen sink

- Unexpected cost: $1,200 for subfloor replacement
- Timeline delay: 3 days

Week 7: City inspector required permit for electrical work

- Unexpected cost: $600 in permits and re-inspection fees

- Timeline delay: 1 week

By month two, Elliot's $23,000 renovation budget had grown to $28,000, and his 4-month timeline was looking more like 5-6 months.

"Welcome to flipping," Marcus laughed when Elliot called him in frustration. "Your first project always costs more and takes longer than expected. The key is learning from each one."

THE LEARNING CURVE

Despite the setbacks, Elliot was learning valuable lessons:

Project Management Skills:

- How to coordinate multiple contractors
- The importance of detailed contracts and timelines
- Building in buffer time and budget for unknowns

Construction Knowledge:

- What renovations add value vs. what's just expensive
- How to spot potential problems during initial walkthrough
- The difference between cosmetic issues and structural problems

Market Understanding:

- What buyers in his target demographic actually wanted
- How staging and photography affected sale price and timeline
- The importance of pricing strategy and timing

More importantly, he was developing confidence in his ability to create value through his own efforts rather than just relying on market appreciation.

YOUR HOUSE FLIPPING ACTION PLAN

STEP 1: Educate Yourself Before You Start

Essential Knowledge Areas:

- Basic construction and renovation processes
- Local permit requirements and building codes
- Market analysis and comparable sales research
- Contractor vetting and project management

Resources for Learning:

- BiggerPockets house flipping calculator and forums
- Local real estate investment meetups
- YouTube channels showing actual renovation projects

- Home improvement stores' weekend workshops

STEP 2: Analyze Your Target Market

Research Requirements:

- Study recent sales in 3-5 target neighborhoods
- Identify what buyers in each area value most
- Calculate average renovation costs per square foot
- Understand seasonal market patterns

Key Metrics to Track:

- Average days on market for renovated vs. unrenovated homes
- Price premium for updates (kitchen, bathrooms, flooring)
- Minimum and maximum price points that sell quickly
- Competition from other flippers and new construction

STEP 3: Build Your Team Before You Need Them

Essential Team Members:

- Real estate agent specializing in investment properties

- General contractor or multiple specialty contractors
- Hard money lender or alternative financing source
- Accountant familiar with real estate tax implications
- Property inspector with construction experience

Vetting Process:

- Get references from recent projects
- Visit job sites to see work quality
- Verify licenses and insurance
- Start with smaller projects to test reliability

STEP 4: Run Conservative Numbers on Every Deal

The 70% Rule:

- Maximum offer = (After Repair Value × 70%) - Renovation Costs
- Example: $140,000 ARV × 70% = $98,000 - $25,000 renovation = $73,000 max offer

Buffer Planning:

- Add 20% to renovation cost estimates
- Add 25% to timeline estimates
- Plan for 6 months of holding costs minimum

- Keep 10% of project cost as contingency fund

THE SALE AND LESSONS LEARNED

Five and a half months after purchase, Elliot's flip was ready for market. The transformation was dramatic—the dated ranch had become a modern, move-in-ready home that showed beautifully.

Final Numbers:

- Purchase price: $89,000
- Actual renovation costs: $29,500
- Holding costs: $5,500
- Selling costs: $8,700
- **Total investment: $132,700**
- **Sale price: $142,000**
- **Net profit: $9,300**

The profit was lower than projected, but Elliot had learned invaluable lessons worth far more than the $9,300 he'd made:

Key Insights:

- Always budget 20-25% above estimates for unexpected costs
- Time is money—delays cost more than most people realize

- The right contractor is worth paying more for
- Market timing matters—winter sales take longer
- Systems and checklists prevent costly mistakes

More importantly, he'd proven to himself that he could successfully complete a real estate project from start to finish.

THE PATH FORWARD

That evening, Elliot updated his financial spreadsheet. The flip had generated a 28% return on his invested capital in 5.5 months—not spectacular, but solid for a first project.

But as he sat in the newly renovated kitchen, eating takeout Chinese food before the final walkthrough tomorrow, Elliot realized something important: while flipping had been profitable and educational, it wasn't scalable in the way he needed for his $2 million goal.

Flipping was trading his time and effort for money—more lucrative than his day job, but still fundamentally limited by how many projects he could personally manage.

His phone buzzed with a text from Marcus: "Congrats on finishing your first flip! Ready to talk about buy-and-hold properties? I found a duplex that might interest you."

Elliot smiled. Phase one of his real estate education was complete. Phase two—building passive income through rental properties—was about to begin.

In our next chapter, we'll follow Elliot as he transitions from flipping houses for short-term profits to building a rental property portfolio for long-term passive income—learning the fundamentals of cash flow analysis and property management.

Chapter 7

BUILDING YOUR OWN MONEY MACHINE - STARTING A BUSINESS

THE PASSIVE INCOME REVELATION

Three weeks after selling his first flip, Elliot sat across from Marcus at their favorite coffee shop, listening to something that would fundamentally change his approach to wealth building.

"The flip was great for learning," Marcus said, "but it's not going to get you to $2 million by 40. You made $9,300 in five months, which is solid, but you traded your time for that money. What if I told you there was a way to make money while you sleep?"

Marcus pulled out his phone and showed Elliot a banking app. "Look at this deposit from yesterday: $2,400. That's my monthly rental income from three properties. I didn't lift a finger for it."

"But don't you have to deal with tenants, repairs, maintenance?"

"Sure, but I hire a property management company for 10% of the rent. They handle everything—tenant screening, rent collection, maintenance calls, even evictions if needed. My properties literally run themselves."

Elliot studied the numbers Marcus was showing him. Three duplexes generating $2,400 per month in net cash flow, with total down payments of $75,000. That was a 38% annual return on invested capital, and it was passive.

"The best part," Marcus continued, "is that it compounds. Every dollar of cash flow I don't spend goes toward buying the next property. And the tenants are paying down my mortgages every month, building equity I didn't pay for."

THE DUPLEX DISCOVERY

Marcus had been tracking a duplex in the Riverside Heights neighborhood — the same area where Elliot had completed his flip. The owner was an elderly man who'd owned the property for thirty years and wanted to cash out for retirement.

"Come look at it with me," Marcus suggested. "Even if you're not ready to buy, you should understand how rental property analysis works."

The duplex was a solid brick building from 1985, well-maintained with separate utilities for each unit. Both sides were currently rented to long-term tenants paying $850 per month each.

Property Details:

- Two 2-bedroom, 1-bathroom units
- Separate entrances and utilities

- Off-street parking for four cars
- Recent updates: roof (2018), HVAC systems (2019)
- Current gross income: $1,700/month

The asking price was $165,000, which seemed high until Marcus walked Elliot through the analysis.

"Don't think like a homebuyer," Marcus explained. "Think like a business investor. This property generates $20,400 per year in income. What other investment gives you a 12% return with built-in inflation protection?"

But the real magic was in the financing structure.

THE POWER OF LEVERAGE

Marcus introduced Elliot to a concept that would become central to his wealth-building strategy: leverage.

"With stocks, if you want to own $100,000 worth of Apple shares, you need $100,000 in cash," Marcus explained. "But with real estate, you can control $165,000 worth of property with just $33,000 down."

The Leverage Math:

- Property value: $165,000
- Down payment (20%): $33,000
- Mortgage amount: $132,000

- Loan terms: 30 years at 5.5% interest

"The bank is essentially partnering with you," Marcus continued. "They put up 80% of the money, but you get 100% of the appreciation and cash flow. And the tenants pay the mortgage for you."

Elliot was starting to understand why Marcus had pivoted from flipping to rental properties. Flipping required his constant involvement and generated one-time profits. Rental properties generated ongoing income with minimal time investment.

THE CASH FLOW ANALYSIS

That evening, Elliot created a detailed cash flow analysis using the frameworks Marcus had taught him:

Monthly Income:

- Unit A rent: $850
- Unit B rent: $850
- **Gross monthly income: $1,700**

Monthly Expenses:

- Mortgage payment (P&I): $875
- Property taxes: $200
- Insurance: $125
- Property management (10%): $170
- Maintenance reserve: $150

- Vacancy allowance (5%): $85
- **Total monthly expenses: $1,605**

Net Monthly Cash Flow: $95

At first glance, $95 per month seemed disappointing—barely a 3.5% return on his $33,000 down payment. But Marcus had taught him to look at the complete picture.

Total Annual Return Analysis:

- Cash flow: $1,140 (12 × $95)
- Principal paydown: $1,800 (tenants paying mortgage)
- Estimated appreciation (3%): $4,950
- Tax benefits (depreciation): $2,000
- **Total annual return: $9,890**

When factored holistically, the duplex would generate a 30% return on his invested capital in the first year, with income that increased annually through rent raises and mortgage paydown.

THE FINANCING CHALLENGE

Despite the attractive returns, Elliot faced a significant challenge: qualifying for an investment property loan was more complex than his flip financing.

Investment property mortgages required:

- 20-25% down payment

- Higher interest rates than owner-occupied properties
- Proof of rental income potential
- Strong credit score and debt-to-income ratios
- Six months of mortgage payments in reserves

His CPA income and growing investment portfolio helped, but lenders were conservative about first-time rental property investors.

After meeting with three lenders, Elliot found a local bank that specialized in investment properties. The loan officer walked him through their requirements:

"For your first rental property, we'll need 25% down plus closing costs. That's about $41,000 total. We'll also need to see six months of payments in reserves—another $10,000. Are you comfortable with that level of investment?"

Elliot did the math. $51,000 represented about 20% of his total net worth. It was a substantial commitment, but the numbers supported the decision.

DUE DILIGENCE AND NEGOTIATION

Before committing $51,000, Elliot conducted thorough due diligence:

Property Inspection:

- Hired a professional inspector with rental property experience

- Found minor issues: some plumbing updates needed ($1,200)
- Overall condition: good maintenance, solid structure

Market Analysis:

- Researched comparable rentals in the area
- Current rents were slightly below market ($875 vs. $900)
- Strong rental demand in the neighborhood

Tenant Review:

- Both tenants had 2+ year rental histories
- On-time rent payments documented
- Leases transferring to new owner

Financial Verification:

- Reviewed two years of income and expense statements
- Confirmed property tax assessments
- Verified insurance costs

Armed with this information, Elliot made an offer: $158,000 with the seller covering closing costs and the $1,200 plumbing repairs.

After three days of negotiation, they settled at $160,000 with seller concessions of $3,000.

THE PROPERTY MANAGEMENT DECISION

One of Elliot's biggest decisions was whether to manage the property himself or hire a management company.

Self-Management Pros:

- Save 10% management fee ($170/month)
- Direct control over tenant selection and maintenance
- Learn the business hands-on

Self-Management Cons:

- Time commitment for showing units, collecting rent, handling repairs
- 24/7 responsibility for emergency calls
- Legal liability and tenant relations stress

Professional Management Pros:

- Experienced tenant screening and placement
- Established contractor relationships
- Legal expertise and eviction procedures
- Truly passive income

Professional Management Cons:

- 10% of gross rents ($170/month)
- Less direct control over decisions

- Potential for higher maintenance costs

Given his demanding day job and growing consulting practice, Elliot chose professional management. The $170 monthly fee was worth the peace of mind and time savings.

THE FIRST YEAR EXPERIENCE

Elliot's first year as a rental property owner was educational and profitable:

Month 1-3: Smooth transition

- Both existing tenants stayed
- Property management company handled minor maintenance issues
- Cash flow consistent at $95/month

Month 4: First vacancy

- Tenant A gave 30-day notice
- Unit vacant for 3 weeks during turnover
- Property management found new tenant at $900/month

Month 7: Major repair

- Water heater replacement needed: $1,200
- Dipped into maintenance reserves
- Reminded Elliot why reserves were essential

Month 10: Rent increase

- Tenant B accepted $50/month increase to $900
- Both units now at market rates

Year-End Financial Summary:

- Total rent collected: $20,100
- Operating expenses: $18,200
- Net cash flow: $1,900
- Principal paydown: $1,850
- Estimated appreciation: $4,800
- **Total return: $8,550 (21% on invested capital)**

THE SCALING STRATEGY

By the end of year one, Elliot understood the power of rental real estate. The duplex had generated returns that exceeded his stock portfolio while providing diversification and inflation protection.

More importantly, he'd learned the systems and processes needed to scale:

Refinement Areas:

- Better initial tenant screening to reduce turnover
- Building relationships with reliable contractors
- Understanding which improvements added value vs. unnecessary expenses
- Optimizing the balance between cash flow and appreciation

Scaling Plan:

- Purchase one property per year for the next five years
- Focus on similar duplex and small multifamily properties
- Build relationships with wholesalers and off-market deal sources
- Eventually transition to larger apartment complexes

The phone rang, interrupting his planning session. It was his property management company.

"Elliot, we have some good news. The property next door to your duplex just came on the market. The owner wants to sell quickly. Are you interested in taking a look?"

YOUR RENTAL PROPERTY ACTION PLAN

STEP 1: Master the Financial Analysis

Key Metrics to Calculate:

- **Cash-on-cash return:** Annual cash flow ÷ total cash invested
- **Cap rate:** Net operating income ÷ purchase price
- **Gross rent multiplier:** Purchase price ÷ gross annual rent

- **Debt coverage ratio:** Net operating income ÷ annual debt service

The 1% Rule:

- Monthly rent should equal 1% of purchase price
- Example: $150,000 property should rent for $1,500/month
- Harder to find but good screening tool

STEP 2: Understand Your Financing Options

Conventional Investment Loans:

- 20-25% down payment required
- Higher interest rates than owner-occupied
- Stricter qualification requirements
- Need 2-6 months of payments in reserves

Alternative Financing:

- Portfolio lenders (keep loans in-house)
- Hard money for fix-and-rent projects
- Owner financing arrangements
- Partnership structures

STEP 3: Build Your Investment Criteria

Property Type Focus:

- Single-family homes in good school districts

- Small multifamily (2-4 units) for better cash flow
- Focus on one geographic area initially
- Target specific price ranges and property conditions

Market Selection Criteria:

- Strong job growth and population trends
- Diverse employment base
- Good landlord-tenant laws
- Active rental market with low vacancy rates

STEP 4: Assemble Your Team

Essential Team Members:

- Real estate agent specializing in investment properties
- Property management company (interview multiple)
- Accountant with real estate experience
- Reliable contractors for maintenance and improvements
- Insurance agent familiar with rental properties

Property Management Evaluation:

- Fee structure (typically 8-12% of gross rents)
- Tenant screening process and criteria

- Maintenance coordination and markup policies
- Financial reporting and rent collection procedures

THE BUSINESS MINDSET SHIFT

Six months into owning the duplex, Elliot experienced a fundamental mindset shift. He stopped thinking like someone who had a job and started thinking like someone who owned businesses.

The duplex wasn't just an investment—it was a small business that generated revenue, had operating expenses, and required strategic management. The monthly cash flow statements weren't just numbers—they were profit and loss reports for his real estate company.

This shift in thinking affected every financial decision he made:

- Should he buy a new car? Only if it helped his business (tax deduction for property visits)
- Should he take a vacation? Factor in the opportunity cost of not looking at deals
- Should he spend money on education? Absolutely, if it improved his investing skills

Marcus noticed the change during one of their coffee meetings. "You're starting to think like an investor instead of an employee. That's the difference between people who build wealth and people who just accumulate savings."

"What do you mean?"

"Employees think about monthly budgets and annual salaries. Investors think about cash flow, returns on investment, and asset allocation. You're starting to see money as a tool rather than something to spend."

Elliot's phone buzzed with a rental income notification: $1,800 deposited automatically. Money he'd earned while sleeping.

For the first time, he truly understood what passive income meant. And he wanted more of it.

But as his rental portfolio grew, Elliot was beginning to realize that small residential properties had limitations. The next level of real estate investing—commercial properties—offered the potential for larger deals, better returns, and true scalability.

In our next chapter, we'll follow Elliot as he makes the leap to commercial real estate investing, learning how to analyze apartment complexes and office buildings while discovering the power of institutional-quality investments.

Chapter 8

BECOMING THE BANK - CAPITAL INVESTING

THE COMMERCIAL REAL ESTATE INTRODUCTION

Two years after purchasing his first duplex, Elliot had built a small but profitable rental portfolio: three duplex properties generating $4,200 monthly in net cash flow. At 28 years old, his net worth had crossed $400,000, with $150,000 in real estate equity and $250,000 in stock investments.

But he was hitting a ceiling. Finding good duplex deals had become increasingly difficult as more investors crowded into the small multifamily market. The properties that penciled out required more and more capital for smaller and smaller returns.

The breakthrough came during a commercial real estate conference Marcus had convinced him to attend.

"You're thinking too small," said Janet Morrison, a commercial real estate broker with twenty years of experience. She was presenting on apartment complex investing to a room full of small-time landlords. "You're competing with every rookie investor for duplex deals, but commercial properties have higher barriers to entry—which means less competition and better returns."

Janet pulled up a slide showing a 24-unit apartment complex she'd recently sold.

Property Details:

- 24 units, average rent $1,200/month
- Gross annual income: $345,600
- Net operating income: $248,832
- Sale price: $3,200,000
- Investor down payment: $800,000
- Annual cash flow: $165,000

"This investor put down $800,000 and generates $165,000 annually in cash flow—a 20.6% cash-on-cash return. Plus, commercial properties are valued based on income, not comparable sales. Improve the income, and you force appreciation."

Elliot's mind raced. $165,000 annually was more than his current salary and consulting income combined. But $800,000 down payment was sixteen times larger than his duplex investments.

After the presentation, he approached Janet with the obvious question: "How does someone like me, with limited capital, get into commercial deals?"

Her answer would change his investment trajectory forever.

THE SYNDICATION EDUCATION

"You don't need $800,000," Janet explained. "You need to understand syndications."

She handed him a business card for Marcus Wells, a local syndicator (not his friend Marcus, but a coincidental name match). "Marcus puts together investment groups for commercial properties. Individual investors contribute $50,000-100,000 each, and together they buy apartment complexes and office buildings."

"How does that work exactly?"

"Think of it like a private mutual fund for real estate. Marcus finds the property, analyzes the deal, arranges financing, and manages the investment. You contribute capital and receive quarterly distributions plus a share of the profits when the property sells."

That weekend, Elliot attended an investor education seminar hosted by Marcus Wells. The room was filled with high-net-worth individuals—doctors, lawyers, business owners—all looking for alternatives to stock market investing.

The Syndication Structure:

- **General Partner (GP):** Finds deals, manages properties, makes decisions
- **Limited Partners (LPs):** Provide capital, receive passive returns

- **Typical minimums:** $50,000-100,000 per deal
- **Target returns:** 12-18% annually for LPs
- **Time horizon:** 3-7 years per investment

Marcus Wells walked through a current deal: a 36-unit apartment complex in a growing suburb.

Deal Overview:

- Purchase price: $4.8 million
- Total equity needed: $1.2 million
- Investor minimum: $75,000
- Projected annual return: 14% to limited partners
- Hold period: 5 years
- Projected total return: 95% over 5 years

"We're not just buying an apartment complex," Marcus explained. "We're buying a business. Our plan is to improve operations, increase rents, and force appreciation through value creation."

THE BUSINESS PLAN ANALYSIS

The syndication's business plan was sophisticated and data-driven:

Value Creation Strategy:

1. **Operational improvements:** Professional management, better tenant screening

2. **Physical improvements:** Unit renovations to justify higher rents
3. **Expense optimization:** Energy efficiency, bulk purchasing, technology
4. **Market positioning:** Rebranding and improved tenant amenities

Financial Projections:

- **Year 1:** $125,000 annual cash flow for all investors (10.4% distribution)
- **Years 2-3:** Rent increases and improved occupancy boost cash flow
- **Year 4-5:** Major value-add renovations increase property value
- **Exit strategy:** Refinance or sell at higher valuation

The sophistication was appealing, but Elliot had learned to be skeptical of projections. He spent the next month conducting due diligence:

Market Research:

- Studied comparable apartment complexes in the area
- Analyzed rental rates and occupancy trends
- Researched employment and population growth
- Evaluated the general partner's track record

Financial Analysis:

- Stress-tested projections with conservative assumptions
- Calculated potential returns under various scenarios
- Compared to his current duplex investments
- Evaluated liquidity considerations (money tied up for 5 years)

The numbers checked out, but the minimum investment of $75,000 represented nearly half his available cash. This would be his largest single investment to date.

THE INVESTMENT DECISION

Elliot called Robert Chen, his longtime mentor, to discuss the opportunity.

"Commercial real estate syndications can be excellent investments," Robert said, "but they're fundamentally different from your duplex properties. You're giving up control in exchange for professional management and larger scale."

"Is that good or bad?"

"It depends on your goals. With your duplexes, you're the general partner—you make all the decisions and keep all the profits. With syndications, you're a limited partner—you provide capital and receive returns, but someone else makes the decisions."

Robert helped him think through the pros and cons:

Syndication Advantages:

- Access to larger, higher-quality properties
- Professional management and expertise
- Diversification across multiple properties
- Passive investment requiring no time
- Potential for higher returns than small properties

Syndication Disadvantages:

- Less control over investment decisions
- Illiquid investment (money tied up for years)
- Dependence on general partner's competence and integrity
- Higher minimum investments
- Complex legal structures and tax implications

"The key question," Robert concluded, "is whether this fits your overall wealth-building strategy. Are you trying to build a real estate business or a diversified investment portfolio?"

THE PORTFOLIO ALLOCATION STRATEGY

That question forced Elliot to step back and evaluate his entire financial picture. At 28, his wealth allocation was:

- Stock investments: $250,000 (62%)
- Real estate equity: $150,000 (38%)
- Cash reserves: $50,000

His goal was $2 million by age 40 — twelve years to accumulate $1.6 million more. At his current savings rate of $60,000 annually, he needed his investments to compound at about 15% annually to reach his target.

The syndication offered potentially higher returns than his duplex investments, but with different risk characteristics. After extensive analysis, Elliot decided to invest $75,000 in the apartment complex syndication.

His reasoning:

- Diversification beyond small residential properties
- Professional management and expertise
- Potential for superior returns
- Learning opportunity for future commercial investments
- Still maintaining his duplex properties for control and cash flow

THE INVESTMENT PROCESS

Investing in the syndication was significantly more complex than buying duplex properties:

Legal Documentation:

- Private Placement Memorandum (100+ pages of deal details and risks)
- Operating Agreement (defining investor rights and responsibilities)
- Subscription Agreement (formal investment commitment)
- Accredited investor verification

Due Diligence Period:

- Property inspection reports and environmental assessments
- Market studies and rent comparisons
- Third-party appraisal and property valuation
- General partner background checks and references

Investment Timeline:

- **Week 1-2:** Review all documentation and conduct due diligence
- **Week 3:** Submit investment commitment and wire funds to escrow

- **Week 4:** Closing and official partnership formation
- **Ongoing:** Quarterly reports and annual tax documentation

The process took a month from initial commitment to closing, compared to 30-45 days for his duplex purchases.

FIRST YEAR PERFORMANCE

Elliot's first year as a commercial real estate limited partner exceeded expectations:

Quarterly Distributions:

- Q1: $1,950 (10.4% annualized)
- Q2: $2,025 (10.8% annualized)
- Q3: $2,100 (11.2% annualized)
- Q4: $2,250 (12.0% annualized)

Total Year 1 Return: $8,325 (11.1% cash-on-cash)

The increasing distributions reflected the general partner's successful implementation of their business plan. Occupancy had improved from 85% to 94%, and average rents had increased by $75 per unit through strategic improvements.

More importantly, the investment was truly passive. While his duplex properties required ongoing attention—approving repairs, reviewing tenant applications, monitoring property management — the syndication required nothing beyond reviewing quarterly reports.

THE LEARNING AND NETWORKING EFFECT

The commercial real estate investment opened doors Elliot hadn't expected. Marcus Wells invited all limited partners to quarterly investor meetings, where they shared market insights and upcoming opportunities.

At these meetings, Elliot met other serious investors:

Dr. Sarah Kim: Emergency room physician investing $100,000+ annually in syndications
James Rodriguez: Business owner who'd built a $2 million portfolio through commercial real estate
Lisa Chen: Tech executive using syndications to diversify away from company stock

These relationships provided education and future investment opportunities. More importantly, they exposed Elliot to different wealth-building strategies and mindsets.

"The biggest difference between small and large investors," James told him, "isn't the amount of money they have — it's how they think about money. Small investors focus on saving. Large investors focus on investing in assets that produce income."

YOUR COMMERCIAL REAL ESTATE ACTION PLAN

STEP 1: Understand Syndication Structures

Key Terms to Learn:

- **General Partner (GP):** Manages the investment and operations
- **Limited Partner (LP):** Provides capital, receives passive returns
- **Preferred return:** Minimum return to LPs before GP receives profits
- **Waterfall structure:** How profits are split between GPs and LPs

Common Investment Types:

- Apartment complexes (multifamily)
- Office buildings
- Retail centers
- Industrial warehouses
- Self-storage facilities

STEP 2: Evaluate General Partners

Due Diligence Checklist:

- Track record with previous investments
- Experience in target property types and markets
- Financial stability and reputation

- Alignment of interests (GP investment in deals)
- Communication and reporting practices

Red Flags to Avoid:

- Unrealistic return projections (>20% annually)
- Lack of transparency in reporting
- General partners with limited experience
- Deals with insufficient cash reserves
- High fees or unfavorable profit splits

STEP 3: Analyze Investment Opportunities

Key Metrics to Evaluate:

- **Cash-on-cash return:** Annual cash flow ÷ initial investment
- **IRR (Internal Rate of Return):** Annualized return including cash flow and appreciation
- **Equity multiple:** Total returns ÷ initial investment over hold period
- **Debt coverage ratio:** Property income ÷ debt service

Market Analysis Requirements:

- Local employment and population trends
- Comparable property sales and rental rates
- Supply and demand dynamics

- Regulatory environment and tax implications

STEP 4: Build Your Investment Portfolio

Diversification Strategy:

- Geographic diversification across markets
- Property type diversification (multifamily, office, retail)
- General partner diversification
- Hold period diversification (some shorter, some longer-term)

Capital Allocation Approach:

- Start with 10-20% of investment portfolio in syndications
- Gradually increase allocation as you gain experience
- Maintain liquidity for unexpected opportunities
- Balance passive syndications with direct real estate ownership

THE WEALTH ACCELERATION EFFECT

Two years after his first commercial syndication, Elliot had invested in four different deals totaling $275,000. His commercial real estate portfolio was generating $32,000 annually in passive income while building equity through property appreciation and mortgage paydown.

His overall real estate portfolio now included:

- Three duplex properties: $6,000 annual cash flow
- Four commercial syndications: $32,000 annual distributions
- **Total real estate income: $38,000 annually**

At age 30, Elliot's net worth had reached $650,000:

- Stock investments: $320,000
- Real estate equity: $330,000
- Cash reserves: $75,000

The commercial investments had accelerated his wealth building significantly. More importantly, they'd educated him about institutional-quality real estate and connected him with other serious investors.

But Elliot was beginning to realize that even commercial real estate syndications had limitations. He was still fundamentally a passive investor, dependent on others' decisions and expertise.

His phone rang, interrupting his quarterly portfolio review. It was Marcus Wells with an intriguing opportunity.

"Elliot, I have something different for you. Instead of being a limited partner in our next deal, we're looking for someone to partner with us as a general partner. You'd bring capital and help with investor relations. Interested in learning more?"

The opportunity to transition from passive investor to active deal sponsor was appealing, but it would require a completely different level of involvement and expertise.

As Elliot considered the opportunity, he realized he was approaching another inflection point in his wealth-building journey. He'd mastered employee income, aggressive saving, stock investing, small real estate deals, and passive commercial investments.

The next level wasn't just about finding better investments—it was about becoming the person who created those investment opportunities for others.

In our next chapter, we'll follow Elliot as he explores the transition from investor to entrepreneur, learning how to build scalable businesses and become a source of investment opportunities rather than just a consumer of them.

Chapter 9

THE FINAL SPRINT - OPTIMIZING YOUR WEALTH MACHINE

THE ENTREPRENEUR'S AWAKENING

At 30 years old, Elliot stood in his home office reviewing his quarterly net worth statement: $650,000. In eight years, he'd gone from living in his parents' basement with negative net worth to building a diversified investment portfolio that generated $75,000 annually in passive income.

But as he stared at the numbers, a sobering realization hit him: he needed $1.35 million more in the next ten years to reach his $2 million goal by 40. At his current pace, he'd fall short by about $300,000.

The math was unforgiving. Even with his aggressive saving rate and strong investment returns, traditional wealth-building strategies alone wouldn't get him to his goal. He needed to think bigger.

The answer came during a conversation with Marcus Wells about the general partnership opportunity.

"The real money in real estate isn't in being an investor," Marcus explained. "It's in being the person who creates the investment opportunities. When I syndicate a deal, I earn acquisition fees, management fees, and a share of all profits. On a $5 million property, that could be $500,000+ over five years."

"But I don't have the experience to sponsor commercial deals."

"You don't need to start with commercial real estate. Start with what you know. You understand duplex investments, tax consulting, and financial planning. Each of those could become a scalable business."

That conversation planted a seed that would transform Elliot's approach to wealth building.

THE BUSINESS MODEL REVELATION

Over the next month, Elliot analyzed his current income sources with fresh eyes:

Current Income Streams:

- Day job salary: $78,000
- Tax consulting: $45,000 (seasonal, time-intensive)
- Real estate cash flow: $38,000 (passive)
- Investment dividends: $12,000 (passive)
- **Total: $173,000 annually**

The problem was scalability. His day job had limited upside. His tax consulting traded time for money. Only his investments scaled without additional time investment.

But what if he could build businesses that generated income without requiring his constant presence?

Business Model Analysis:

- **Tax consulting:** Could he hire other CPAs and take a percentage of their revenue?
- **Real estate:** Could he help others invest in rental properties and earn fees?
- **Financial planning:** Could he monetize his wealth-building knowledge?

The entrepreneur inside him was awakening.

THE TAX BUSINESS SCALING STRATEGY

Elliot's first entrepreneurial venture grew organically from his existing tax consulting practice. He'd been turning away clients during tax season because he couldn't handle the volume alone.

Instead of continuing to turn away business, he decided to hire help.

Martinez Tax Solutions Expansion:

- Hired two part-time CPAs during tax season
- Elliot handled complex returns and business development
- Associates handled individual returns under his supervision
- Revenue sharing: 60% to associate, 40% to Elliot

The model worked brilliantly. In the first expanded tax season:

- Total revenue: $125,000 (vs. $45,000 previous year)
- Elliot's direct work: $55,000
- Management and oversight income: $28,000
- **Net increase in Elliot's income: $38,000**

More importantly, he'd learned to generate income from others' work—the fundamental principle of business ownership.

THE REAL ESTATE EDUCATION BUSINESS

Elliot's success with duplex investing had attracted attention from other would-be investors. Friends, coworkers, and even strangers at real estate meetups regularly asked for advice.

"You should charge for this knowledge," suggested Dr. Sarah Kim, his syndication colleague. "I'd have paid $5,000 to learn what you know about rental property analysis before I made my first investment mistakes."

That comment sparked an idea. Elliot began developing a real estate investment education business:

"Duplex Wealth Academy" Business Model:

- Weekend workshops: $500 per person, 20 participants = $10,000 per event

- Online course: $1,500, target 100 students annually = $150,000
- One-on-one coaching: $200/hour, 10 hours per month = $24,000 annually
- Deal analysis service: $500 per property analysis

The first workshop sold out in two weeks. Participants included doctors, lawyers, and business owners—all high-income professionals who lacked real estate knowledge.

"This is exactly what I needed," said workshop participant Jennifer Martinez, a software engineer. "I've been intimidated by real estate investing, but your systematic approach makes it feel manageable."

The positive feedback confirmed Elliot was onto something significant.

THE WEALTH MANAGEMENT CONSULTING EVOLUTION

Elliot's third business emerged from his comprehensive approach to wealth building. Many high-income professionals excelled in their careers but struggled with investment strategy and tax optimization.

Comprehensive Wealth Building Services:

- Investment portfolio analysis and optimization
- Tax strategy and advanced planning
- Real estate investment guidance

- Business structure and asset protection
- Retirement and financial independence planning

He started with three clients, charging $5,000 annually for comprehensive wealth management. Within six months, referrals had grown his client base to twelve families, generating $60,000 in recurring annual revenue.

The beauty of this model was its scalability and recurring nature. Unlike tax prep or real estate transactions, wealth management created ongoing relationships and compound revenue growth.

YOUR ACTION PLAN SUMMARY: THE COMPLETE ROAD MAP TO $2 MILLION BY 40

Before we continue with Elliot's final sprint, let's ensure you have a crystal-clear action plan. Here's everything you must do to reach $2 million by age 40:

PHASE 1: FOUNDATION (Ages 22-25)

Your Mission: Build the foundation for wealth

IMMEDIATE ACTIONS (Do This Week):

1. Calculate your exact net worth using the worksheet from Chapter 1
2. Set up automatic investing - minimum $1,000/month to index funds

3. Implement the 70/30 rule - live on 30% of income, invest 70%

4. Open investment accounts: Vanguard/Fidelity for index funds

5. Start tracking every expense for one month to identify spending leaks

STRATEGIC CAREER MOVES (Do This Quarter):

1. Negotiate your current salary - research market rates and ask for 10-15% increase

2. Develop high-value skills - choose one certification that increases earning potential

3. Launch side income stream - consulting, freelancing, or service business

4. Network strategically - join professional groups in high-income industries

INVESTMENT ALLOCATION:

- 70% US Total Stock Market Index
- 20% International Stock Index
- 10% Bond Index
- **Target: $100,000 invested by age 25**

PHASE 2: ACCELERATION (Ages 25-30)

Your Mission: Scale income and diversify investments

INCOME SCALING (Years 1-2):

1. Maximize tax-advantaged accounts - 401k, IRA, SEP-IRA
2. Build scalable side business - aim for $50,000+ annual revenue
3. Pursue advanced certifications - CPA, CFP, or industry-specific credentials
4. Transition to higher-paying roles - target $75,000+ base salary

REAL ESTATE ENTRY (Years 2-3):

1. Complete real estate education - read 5+ books, attend local meetups
2. Analyze 100+ properties before making first purchase
3. Buy first rental property - focus on cash flow positive duplex
4. Build real estate team - agent, lender, property manager, contractors

PORTFOLIO TARGETS:

- **Age 27:** $250,000 net worth
- **Age 30:** $500,000 net worth
- Real estate: 30-40% of total portfolio

- Monthly passive income: $3,000+

PHASE 3: OPTIMIZATION (Ages 30-35)

Your Mission: Build business systems and scale investments

BUSINESS DEVELOPMENT:

1. Systematize existing income streams - hire others, create processes
2. Develop recurring revenue models - subscriptions, management fees, ongoing services
3. Build commercial real estate portfolio - invest in syndications
4. Consider general partnership opportunities - sponsor deals for higher returns

ADVANCED STRATEGIES:

1. Optimize tax efficiency - advanced strategies saving $10,000+ annually
2. Asset protection planning - LLCs, trusts, insurance strategies
3. International diversification - global real estate and investments
4. Alternative investments - private equity, angel investing, commodities

PORTFOLIO TARGETS:

- **Age 32:** $1,000,000 net worth
- **Age 35:** $1,500,000 net worth
- Monthly passive income: $8,000+

PHASE 4: FINAL SPRINT (Ages 35-40)

Your Mission: Optimize and accelerate to $2 million

WEALTH OPTIMIZATION:

1. Maximize business sale opportunities - sell businesses for lump sum gains
2. Leverage real estate equity - refinance for additional investments
3. Scale commercial investments - larger syndications and direct ownership
4. Optimize withdrawal strategies - prepare for financial independence

CRITICAL SUCCESS FACTORS:

Monthly Investment Requirements by Age:

- Age 22-25: $1,500/month minimum
- Age 25-30: $3,000/month minimum
- Age 30-35: $5,000/month minimum
- Age 35-40: $7,000/month minimum

Income Growth Targets:

- Age 25: $75,000 total annual income

- Age 30: $150,000 total annual income
- Age 35: $250,000 total annual income
- Age 40: Financial independence

The Non-Negotiables (Do These or Fail):

1. Live below your means throughout the entire journey
2. Invest consistently regardless of market conditions
3. Continuously increase your income through skills and business building
4. Diversify across asset classes - stocks, real estate, businesses
5. Reinvest profits instead of lifestyle inflation

ELLIOT'S BUSINESS EMPIRE AT 32

Two years after launching his three businesses, Elliot's financial picture had transformed dramatically:

Business Income (Annual):

- Martinez Tax Solutions: $95,000 (managed team of 4 CPAs)
- Duplex Wealth Academy: $180,000 (online courses + workshops)
- Wealth Management Consulting: $120,000 (20 client families)

- **Total Business Income: $395,000**

Investment Income (Annual):

- Stock dividends: $18,000
- Real estate cash flow: $52,000
- Commercial syndication distributions: $45,000
- **Total Investment Income: $115,000**

Total Annual Income: $510,000

His net worth had exploded to $1.2 million at age 32, putting him ahead of schedule for his $2 million goal.

THE SYSTEMS AND AUTOMATION REVOLUTION

The key to Elliot's success wasn't just building businesses—it was building systems that ran without his constant involvement.

Martinez Tax Solutions Systems:

- Standardized client onboarding process
- Cloud-based document management
- Automated billing and payment processing
- Quality control checklists for all returns
- Performance incentives for associate CPAs

Duplex Wealth Academy Systems:

- Automated email marketing sequences
- Self-paced online learning platform

- Standardized workshop curriculum
- Student success tracking and follow-up
- Affiliate referral program

Wealth Management Systems:
- Comprehensive client intake process
- Quarterly review and reporting templates
- Investment committee decision framework
- Automated rebalancing and tax optimization
- Client portal for 24/7 account access

These systems allowed Elliot to focus on high-value activities: business development, strategic planning, and investment analysis.

THE MINDSET EVOLUTION

By age 32, Elliot had evolved from an employee mindset to an entrepreneur and investor mindset:

Employee Mindset (Age 22):
- Trade time for money
- Focus on job security
- Spend money on lifestyle
- Save what's left over
- Depend on employer for income

Entrepreneur/Investor Mindset (Age 32):

- Build systems that generate income
- Focus on creating value
- Invest money to create more money
- Live below means regardless of income
- Create multiple income streams

This mindset shift was more valuable than any specific strategy or tactic.

THE FINAL ACCELERATION STRATEGY

With $1.2 million at age 32, Elliot needed $800,000 more in eight years—$100,000 annually in net worth growth. Given his income and investment returns, this was achievable, but he developed an acceleration strategy:

Business Optimization:

- Hire general managers for each business
- Develop additional revenue streams within existing businesses
- Consider strategic partnerships or acquisitions
- Explore selling businesses for lump sum capital

Investment Scaling:

- Increase commercial real estate allocation

- Consider private equity and hedge fund investments
- Explore international real estate opportunities
- Potentially sponsor commercial real estate deals

Tax Optimization:

- Advanced retirement planning strategies
- Charitable giving for tax benefits
- Business structure optimization
- International tax planning

The phone rang, interrupting his planning session. It was Marcus Wells with the general partnership opportunity he'd been considering.

"Elliot, we're ready to move forward with that apartment complex deal. We need a $200,000 investment from our new general partner, but you'd earn 30% of all profits instead of the typical 8% limited partner return. Interested?"

The opportunity represented a new level of investment sophistication and potential returns. But it also meant risking a significant portion of his liquid net worth.

As he considered the decision, Elliot realized he was no longer the confused college graduate living in his parents' basement. He'd become exactly what he'd set out to become: a sophisticated investor and entrepreneur with multiple income streams and a clear path to financial independence.

The final sprint to $2 million was within reach.

In our final chapter, we'll follow Elliot as he makes the ultimate transition to complete financial independence, learning how to maintain and grow wealth while designing the lifestyle he'd always dreamed of.

Chapter 10

LIVING THE DREAM - YOUR NEW LIFE AT 40

THE MILESTONE MOMENT

Elliot Martinez sat on the deck of his mountain cabin, laptop open, reviewing his quarterly portfolio statement. The date was March 15th—three months past his 40th birthday. The number at the bottom of the screen made him smile: **Net Worth: $2,247,000**.

He'd done it. Eighteen years after living in his parents' basement with negative net worth, he had achieved complete financial independence.

But the journey to this moment hadn't been linear. The final eight years had included market crashes, business setbacks, family emergencies, and moments of doubt. The path from $1.2 million at age 32 to over $2 million at 40 had required every lesson he'd learned about resilience, adaptation, and long-term thinking.

The Final Numbers:

- Stock investments: $450,000
- Real estate equity: $650,000
- Business valuations: $800,000
- Commercial real estate syndications: $347,000

- **Total Net Worth: $2,247,000**

Annual Passive Income:

- Investment dividends: $22,000
- Real estate cash flow: $78,000
- Business distributions: $185,000
- Commercial syndication returns: $52,000
- **Total Annual Income: $337,000**

More importantly, this income required virtually no active work from Elliot. His businesses ran themselves through the systems he'd built. His real estate generated cash flow through professional management. His investments compounded automatically through reinvestment.

He was financially free.

THE FINAL SPRINT CHALLENGES (AGES 32-40)

The last eight years had tested every aspect of Elliot's wealth-building knowledge and emotional resilience.

The 2025 Market Correction (Age 33)

Just one year after reaching $1.2 million, the stock market crashed 35% in six months. Elliot watched $400,000 of his net worth evaporate in four weeks.

"This is why we diversify," Robert Chen had reminded him during their emergency coffee meeting. "And this is why we don't panic."

Instead of selling, Elliot did something that felt counterintuitive but proved brilliant: he increased his investments. Using cash flow from his businesses, he bought more index funds at discounted prices.

"When stocks are on sale, you buy more, not less," he reminded himself, echoing lessons from his first market downturn years earlier.

The recovery took two years, but his additional purchases during the crash generated outsized returns when the market rebounded.

The Business Partnership Disaster (Age 35)

Elliot's decision to partner with Marcus Wells on a commercial real estate deal nearly derailed his progress. The $200,000 general partnership investment in a 48-unit apartment complex turned into a nightmare when the property management company embezzled funds and several major repairs depleted reserves.

For eighteen months, the property generated negative cash flow while Elliot and his partners injected additional capital to stabilize operations. His $200,000 investment grew to $280,000 before the situation was resolved.

"Even good deals with good partners can go wrong," he learned. "The key is having enough diversification that no single investment can destroy your overall plan."

The property eventually stabilized and sold for a modest profit, but the experience taught Elliot valuable lessons about due diligence, reserve planning, and risk management.

The Family Emergency Fund Test (Age 37)

When Elliot's father suffered a heart attack and required expensive medical treatment not covered by insurance, Elliot faced his first major unexpected expense: $85,000 for specialized cardiac surgery.

Having maintained substantial cash reserves and emergency funds throughout his wealth-building journey, Elliot could cover the expense without liquidating investments or disrupting his long-term plan.

"Wealth isn't just about accumulating assets," he realized. "It's about having the resources to handle life's unexpected challenges without derailing your financial future."

The experience reinforced the importance of maintaining liquidity and insurance coverage even while pursuing aggressive wealth building.

THE BUSINESS EVOLUTION AND EXIT STRATEGY

By age 38, Elliot's three businesses had grown beyond his wildest projections:

- **Martinez Tax Solutions:** Annual revenue of $400,000 with a team of six CPAs
- **Duplex Wealth Academy:** Annual revenue of $650,000 with online courses, coaching, and live events

- **Wealth Management Consulting:** Annual revenue of $480,000 serving 45 high-net-worth families

But Elliot was also experiencing entrepreneur fatigue. Managing three businesses, even with strong systems, required constant attention and decision-making. He began exploring exit strategies.

The Strategic Sale Process

Working with a business broker, Elliot valued his three companies:

Valuation Methodology:

- Service businesses typically sell for 2-4x annual profit
- Martinez Tax Solutions: $120,000 profit × 3 = $360,000
- Duplex Wealth Academy: $200,000 profit × 4 = $800,000 (recurring revenue premium)
- Wealth Management: $180,000 profit × 3.5 = $630,000

Total Business Value: $1,790,000

The sales process took fourteen months and required careful transition planning to maintain client relationships and business operations.

The Strategic Partial Exit

Rather than selling all three businesses outright, Elliot structured strategic partial exits:

- **Martinez Tax Solutions:** Sold 80% to his lead CPA for $288,000, retained 20% for ongoing passive income

- **Duplex Wealth Academy:** Sold the education components for $600,000, retained real estate consulting for ongoing revenue

- **Wealth Management:** Merged with a larger firm, received $500,000 upfront plus ongoing revenue sharing

Total Proceeds: $1,388,000

The structure allowed Elliot to monetize years of business building while maintaining income streams that required minimal ongoing involvement.

THE INVESTMENT PORTFOLIO OPTIMIZATION

With significant liquidity from business sales, Elliot optimized his investment allocation for financial independence rather than accumulation:

Age 40 Portfolio Allocation *Conservative Growth Focus (40% Stocks, 60% Income-Producing Assets):*

Stock Investments (40% - $450,000):

- Total Stock Market Index: $200,000

- International Stock Index: $150,000

- REIT Index: $100,000

Real Estate (45% - $997,000):

- Direct ownership (5 properties): $650,000
- Commercial syndications: $347,000

Business Interests (15% - $347,000):

- Retained business stakes: $200,000
- Private lending: $147,000

Cash/Fixed Income (5% - $112,000):

- Emergency fund: $50,000
- Short-term bonds: $62,000

This allocation prioritized income generation and stability over growth, reflecting Elliot's transition from wealth accumulation to wealth preservation and income generation.

THE PSYCHOLOGY OF FINANCIAL INDEPENDENCE

Reaching $2 million brought unexpected psychological challenges Elliot hadn't anticipated:

The "What Now?" Syndrome

"I spent eighteen years focused on this goal," Elliot confided to his therapist during his first session after reaching financial independence. "Now that I've achieved it, I feel... empty. What's the point of continuing to work or build wealth?"

This phenomenon—common among early retirees—required Elliot to rediscover purpose beyond financial accumulation.

The Identity Crisis

For nearly two decades, Elliot had defined himself as someone building toward financial independence. When he achieved the goal, he struggled with questions like:

- Who am I if not someone pursuing wealth?
- What motivates me now that money isn't a concern?
- How do I structure my days without work requirements?
- What legacy do I want to create beyond personal wealth?

The Relationship Adjustments

Financial independence also affected Elliot's relationships:

Family Dynamics: His parents struggled to understand his decision to "retire" at 40 when he was successful and earning well.

Friend Relationships: Many friends still focused on careers and accumulating money couldn't relate to his new priorities.

Dating Challenges: Financial independence complicated romantic relationships, requiring careful navigation of money conversations.

DESIGNING THE INDEPENDENT LIFE

After six months of adjustment, Elliot began intentionally designing his post-financial independence lifestyle:

The Purpose Discovery Process

Values Clarification Exercise:

- What activities energize vs. drain me?
- What problems do I want to solve in the world?
- How do I want to spend my limited time on earth?
- What legacy do I want to leave?

The Answers:

- Teaching others about financial independence
- Spending time in nature and outdoor activities
- Building deeper relationships with family and friends

- Contributing to causes larger than personal wealth

The Structured Freedom Approach

Rather than complete retirement, Elliot created "structured freedom":

- **Monday-Wednesday:** Consulting and teaching (by choice, not necessity)
- **Thursday-Friday:** Personal projects and learning
- **Weekends:** Recreation, travel, and relationships

This structure provided purpose and engagement while maintaining the flexibility that financial independence offered.

The Giving Strategy

With financial security assured, Elliot began strategic philanthropy:

- **Annual Giving Budget:** $25,000 (targeting causes aligned with his values)
- **Volunteer Commitment:** 10 hours per week teaching financial literacy
- **Mentorship Program:** Formal mentoring of young professionals pursuing FIRE

YOUR FINANCIAL INDEPENDENCE ACTION PLAN

As you prepare for your own journey to $2 million by 40, here are the final critical strategies:

The 4% Rule and Income Planning

- **Safe Withdrawal Rate:** 4% of investment portfolio annually
- **$2 Million Portfolio:** $80,000 annual safe withdrawal
- **Plus Passive Income:** Real estate and business income
- **Total Available:** $100,000-150,000+ annually

The Pre-Retirement Preparation Checklist

Financial Preparation (Ages 35-40):
☐ Optimize portfolio for income generation over growth
☐ Build 2-3 years of expenses in cash reserves
☐ Ensure health insurance coverage independent of employment
☐ Complete estate planning and asset protection
☐ Test withdrawal strategies and tax efficiency

Psychological Preparation: ☐ Develop hobbies and interests beyond work
☐ Build relationships not centered on career networking
☐ Explore volunteer opportunities and giving strategies
☐ Consider therapy or coaching for transition support
☐ Create structure for post-work life

The Transition Timeline

- **Age 37-38:** Begin reducing work commitments and business dependencies

- **Age 38-39:** Test extended periods away from work (sabbaticals)

- **Age 39-40:** Optimize portfolio for income generation

- **Age 40+:** Transition to financial independence with purpose-driven activities

THE WEALTH LEGACY STRATEGY

With personal financial independence secured, Elliot began focusing on wealth legacy and impact:

The Teaching Mission

- **Duplex Wealth Academy Evolution:** Transitioned from profit-focused to impact-focused education

- **Public Speaking:** Began speaking at conferences about financial independence

- **Writing Project:** Started work on a comprehensive FIRE guidebook

- **YouTube Channel:** Created free educational content reaching 100,000+ subscribers

The Investment Evolution

- **Angel Investing:** Began investing in startups founded by former students and mentees

- **Real Estate Syndication Sponsorship:** Partnered on deals to help others access commercial real estate
- **Private Lending:** Provided capital to real estate investors and small business owners

The Family Wealth Planning

- **Future Family Considerations:** Planned strategies for teaching wealth principles to future children
- **Trust Structures:** Established frameworks for multi-generational wealth transfer
- **Family Mission:** Developed family values around money, work, and contribution

LIVING THE DREAM: A DAY IN THE LIFE

6:00 AM: Wake up naturally (no alarm) in mountain cabin

6:30 AM: Coffee and portfolio review (15 minutes maximum)

7:00 AM: Mountain bike ride or hiking

9:00 AM: Breakfast and planning for the day

10:00 AM: Writing or consulting work (by choice)

12:00 PM: Lunch and rest

2:00 PM: Investment analysis or property visits

4:00 PM: Mentoring call with aspiring FIRE student

5:00 PM: Dinner preparation and relaxation

7:00 PM: Reading, family time, or social activities

9:00 PM: Reflection and gratitude practice

The schedule varied daily, but the common themes were:

- **Choice over obligation** in all activities
- **Impact focus** rather than income focus
- **Balance** between productivity and recreation
- **Relationships** prioritized over transactions

THE FINAL WISDOM

As Elliot reflected on his 18-year journey from broke college graduate to financially independent at 40, several key insights crystallized:

The Success Principles That Made the Difference

1. Start immediately: Time is your most valuable asset in wealth building

2. Live below your means: Lifestyle inflation is the enemy of wealth accumulation

3. Invest aggressively: Conservative investing leads to conservative results

4. Build multiple income streams: Diversification applies to income, not just investments

5. Reinvest profits: Compound interest only works if you let it compound

6. Learn continuously: Knowledge and skills are your highest-return investments

7. Build systems: Create businesses and investments that work without you

8. Stay the course: Markets crash, deals fail, but long-term persistence wins

What Elliot Gained:

- Complete control over his time and activities
- Financial security beyond what employment could provide
- Ability to take risks and pursue passion projects
- Platform to help others achieve similar independence
- Peace of mind about money and the future

THE INVITATION TO BEGIN

As you close this book and consider your own journey to $2 million by 40, remember that Elliot's story began with a simple decision: to live differently than everyone around him.

The strategies, tactics, and frameworks in this book are proven and repeatable. The math works. The investments generate returns. The businesses create value.

But success requires something that no book can provide: the decision to start and the commitment to persist when the journey becomes difficult.

Your journey begins with a single question:

Are you willing to live like most people won't for 18 years so you can live like most people can't for the rest of your life?

If your answer is yes, turn back to Chapter 1 and begin implementing the action steps immediately.

Your future financially independent self is waiting.

The End

EPILOGUE: FIVE YEARS LATER

At age 45, Elliot Martinez had exceeded his wildest expectations. His net worth had grown to $3.2 million through continued investment returns and business income. But more importantly, he'd found deep fulfillment in helping over 1,000 students achieve their own financial independence goals.

His marriage to Dr. Sarah Kim (his former syndication colleague) had brought new dimensions to both their lives. Together, they were building a family foundation focused on financial education and economic mobility.

The cabin where he'd celebrated reaching $2 million had become a retreat center where he hosted financial independence workshops for young professionals.

Most mornings, Elliot still woke up grateful for that decision he'd made at 22 to live below his means and invest aggressively. The compound interest on that decision had generated returns far beyond money—it had created a life of purpose, impact, and freedom.

"The best time to plant a tree was 20 years ago. The second best time is now." - Ancient Proverb

ABOUT THE AUTHOR

Sean Taylor holds a Bachelor of Science in Computer Science with a minor in Mathematics, combining analytical thinking with practical business acumen to decode the mathematics of wealth building.

At 25, he launched his first business, learning firsthand the challenges and rewards of entrepreneurship. A year later, he began investing in real estate, discovering the power of leverage and passive income in building long-term wealth. These early experiences became the foundation for a successful journey in business ownership and real estate investing that would span decades.

Through trial, error, and eventual success, he learned the hard-won lessons that most people discover too late — if at all. While his own path to financial independence extended past age 40, the experience provided invaluable insights into what works, what doesn't, and most importantly, how the journey could be accelerated for those starting earlier.

Today, he shares this knowledge as a real estate investing coach and motivational speaker, helping others overcome the fear and uncertainty that prevent most people from taking their first steps toward financial independence. His speaking engagements focus on building confidence in investing and entrepreneurship—the psychological barriers that often matter more than the technical knowledge.

"How to Retire by 40" represents the culmination of his wealth-building experience, distilled into the systematic approach he wishes he'd had at 22. The strategies in this book aren't theoretical—they're battle-tested methods refined through years of real-world application.

"I wrote this book because I believe everyone deserves the opportunity to achieve financial freedom while they're young enough to truly enjoy it. The traditional path of working until 62 is a choice, not a requirement. This book shows you there's a better way."

His mission is simple: to help as many people as possible escape the paycheck-to-paycheck cycle and design lives of purpose, impact, and freedom—decades ahead of the traditional retirement timeline.

Sean currently coaches real estate investors, speaks at financial independence events, and continues building wealth through the same proven strategies outlined in this book.

www.ingramcontent.com/pod-product-compliance
Lightning Source LLC
Chambersburg PA
CBHW040304170426
43194CB00021B/2885